Brazilian National War College (ESG) in Politics and its Culture: A Study on Military Thinking About the Agrarian Question

HERMES DE ANDRADE JÚNIOR

ISBN-10: 1978106270
ISBN-13: 978-1978106277

DEDICATION

To God be the glory forever and ever. To my wife Tamar, who is my blessing. To my father-in-law and mother-in-law, for your prayers and support. I also offer this book as a gift to my father Hermes for his 80 years old.

CONTENTS

INTRODUCTION

This book covers political studies and military sociology, primarily, although agrarian sociology is on the agenda. The main question that would be asked in the face of such a controversial issue as the Agrarian Question and the relationship with the Armed Forces is: what can be expected from this in the following pages? The curiosity of those who go behind the scenes of agrarian policy by reading the military apparatus happens in these days of invasions and federal interventions in response to the judicial orders of reintegration of possession. Possession of what? Who are the real owners? Where do the popular movements in Brazil today follow and to what extent do the authorities address the problem of social exclusion that goes as a fuse?

These are other typical questions in an atypical country. Although the huge problem that covers them is already known in broad outlines, the solutions are not feasible, in the way things go. The military regime of force gave up. What to do with what's left? Although it no longer exists formally, military thinking still influences institutions, legislation, negotiation mechanisms and security. In this way, knowing more about the military segment is the objective of the work that goes on. In particular, we can see the horizon of the military who planned and implemented a strong national security policy regarding land issues. Sadly, there is no literature available on the subject and it is thought that this dissertation can open a gap before the eyes of researchers interested in deepening the knowledge of the subject, as controversial as the history of Brazil.

But if this pretense exists the difficulties for this are not minor. Some of the sources are still to be unraveled in a way that is better than this, so that you have a more complete work. What is presented is, in fact, a case study when priority publications of the Brazilian National War College (ESG) are examined. Twenty one (21) papers on the agrarian theme were selected, categorized among the students and lecturers of the School, as well as other documents and positions of the School. The methodology adopted allows the reader to enter into the dimension of ESG, through its confrontation with other currents of military thought and with part of the available literature of Brazilian military politics and sociology; and ends with its contextualization with agrarian issues.

Created in 1949 and called the "Brazilian Sorbonne," sometimes ironically, by its detractors, the ESG became increasingly notorious when members of its Permanent Corps and military and civilian trainees occupied key positions of the staff of the government of General Castelo Branco, commander of the School, endorsed President of the Republic and also welcoming of the Statute of the Land in Brazil.
In this way, the institution in question did not call attention only to its courses, but because it constituted a meeting point of politico-economic groups of a military and civil nature. From these premises, understand the ESG's thinking in the military thinking as a whole and in the Brazilian industrial program of the 50's and part of the 60's is an interest; mainly, because there are unfolding of the industrial program in the Project ESG, which was in charge of uniting liberals and conservatives. Industrialism

had consequences for the peasantry. From this unfolding the main conclusions of this study depart and it seems important to map out the agrarian problem, at least in regard to its inconsideration as a problem of society and not only of the authorities, taking into account the so-called cold war and its authoritarianism.

It is necessary to consider the Latin American and world dimension of the conflict, composing a global process of domination. Thus, in the following pages, the essential principles of the Brazilian National Security Doctrine discussed and propagated by the ESG are also registered as a framework of their thinking, since the ESG research methodology is rigidly obeyed.

The design of this work also follows the lines of study of Brazilian authoritarian thinkers: Oliveira Viana, Alberto Torres, among others, since they are well distinguished in the axiological set of ESG. It has always used its democratic vocation, but this paradoxically cannot be reproduced in what is isolated from its discourse.
The study of the oligarchic phenomenon is also relevant to understand the main problems in the North and Northeast of the country in the decades studied. Finally, the ambience to better understand what is characterized as Agrarian Question read by the military segment is being placed and this is the way it is intended to show in these lines.

It will be tried to put as a question that the ESG, as one of the main representatives of the Military Institution, participated actively in the organization of the Brazilian industrialist program and the excessive technicality that encouraged, applied to the Land reforms by the Liberal influence in the approach to the US block in the Cold War, as a complement to this program, did not allow the harmonious development of the damaged areas with the export monoculture, reproducing conflicts that could be better managed.

The chapters follow the order. Chapter 1, The Thinking of The Brazilian National War College (ESG); Chapter 2, The ESG and Currents Of Brazilian Military thinking; Chapter 3, The Agrarian Question as seen by ESG's Doctrine and Chapter 4, The Analysis of the Monographs Produced In ESG
And Conclusion.

1 THE THINKING OF BRAZILIAN NATIONAL WAR COLLEGE ESG

Brief Historical Contextualization and Structuring

In its original conception, the Brazilian National War College (ESG) had the idea of being an Institute of Higher Studies to develop programs for the acquisition and development of knowledge necessary for the direction and planning of national security[1].

At that time, the world had just emerged from World War II, which had involved virtually all the resources of belligerent nations. In addition, nuclear weapons had emerged, generating the Cold War terror climate and the consequent expectation of a third, even more devastating, global conflict.

Brazil had participated in World War II, where it had naturally been strongly influenced by the United States of America, as regards the structure and doctrine of its Armed Forces, apart from other sectors of national life.

In 1946, that country had created the National War College, designed to bring together civilians and the military to study defense problems that were increasingly comprehensive and urgent. To this extent, the United States followed the path begun by Great Britain with the founding of Imperial Defense College in 1927 followed by France with the creation of the Center des *Hautes Études de Défense Nationale* in 1936. The dominant concern in both cases, was the scope of modern warfare[2].

In this way, ESG emerged within such a framework, through the efforts of a group of Brazilian officials who had experienced the great conflict in Europe and identified the need to give greater rationality to government action, aiming to expand the country's defense capacity and consequently, the national security perspective.

Guita Debert[3], commenting on the meaning of the creation of the ESG, points out that three concepts would be understood: total war, starting from the inevitability

---

[1] According to Law 785, of August 20, 1949.

[2] "Jornal do Brasil", Ago 19 1979, in the publication of the article about the 30 years of ESG with CMG Domingos Pacífico Castelo Branco Ferreira, then head of Cabinet of the ESG Command.

[3] Op.cit., pp.85-86.

of a GM that would involve the Western bloc under US hegemony and the Eastern bloc under hegemony of the USSR; that of the unity of the war, where the issue is not only to keep the armed forces united, but to point out the importance of a close relationship between them and the civilians who control from the industry to the mass media. Such a relationship would have proved indispensable in the II World War and is therefore now thought of as a relationship which must be maintained not only in periods of war but also in peace; the internalization of the concept of National Security, since communism comes to be seen not as a threat of an enemy nation, but as an internal enemy that manipulates the existing social tensions in a country for the benefit of its ideology and according to the interests of an enemy nation.

In this context, President Eurico Gaspar Dutra was in favor of the suggestion for the existence of the ESG, issuing orders for the organization of a school of the genre, from the decree of his government marked in October of 1948, designed to minister course of high command to general officers and senior officers of the three armed forces.

This initial conception, however, rapidly evolved into something much more comprehensive, as a result of the work of the committee appointed to organize the School. This is how Cordeiro de Farias, president of the commission, and other commissioners produced a document defining the Fundamental Principles of the Brazilian National War College:

1. National Security is more a function of the nation's general potential than of its Military Potential;
2. Brazil has the basic requirements (area, population, resources), indispensable to become a great power;
3. Brazil's development has been delayed for reasons that may be removed;
4. Like all work, achieving this acceleration (of development) requires the use of a driving energy and a process of applying that energy;
5. The existing impediment to the emergence of national solutions to the Brazilian problems is due to the adopted energy application process and the lack of joint work habits;
6. It is urgent to replace the method of opinions by another method that allows reaching harmonious and balanced solutions; and
7. The instrument to be used for the elaboration of the new method to be adopted and for its diffusion, consists of the creation of a national institute of high studies functioning as a permanent research center[4].

With a critical reading of these fundamentals, the concern is to associate Development Security from the origin of the School, since it points to the improvement of the conditions of National Security through the overall development of the Nation (see principle nr 1).

From this point of view, it was necessary to rethink the national problem also in

---

[4] *Ibid.* With regard to the method of opinions cit. in the sixth "principle", meant, in the understanding of the said commission, as a succession of studies and personalistic solutions that came into conflict causing the paralysis of the public administration. Thus, through criticism of the method, the members of the commission aimed to accelerate the development of the country. On the Fundamental Principles of the Superior School of War, I used the brochure made by the Fleet Admiral Carlos Henrique Resende de Noronha, then Commander of the School (ESG, T1-80, 1980).

conjunction with "civilians of outstanding competence and relevant action in the orientation and execution of the national politics[5]", a fact that is carefully mentioned in the School regulations and that brings about the close cooperation between military and civilians well chosen for the reliable performance of improving the methodology for the formulation and planning of the National Security and Development Policy.

The academic activities of the ESG began in 1950 with the operation of the Superior Course of War (CSG), which has continued without interruption until today, under the full-time regime, annually. This course maintained a balance between military and civilian students, with priority being given to the formation of civilian critical mass. Another ESG school activity, the Military Staff Command and Command Course (CEMCFA) was constituted by the initiative of Juarez Távora when he commanded ESG (1953) and had as its objective the diffusion of the Brazilian Military Doctrine, in particular regarding the exercise of the combined Command and Staff. Subsequent to this, the National Mobilization Course was instituted in 1958, which lasted for an ephemeral period, similar to the first Information Course, which only worked during 1959, and came into being again in 1965 with the creation of the National Information Service (SNI) and again extinct in 1972 by the existence of the National School of Information (EsNI). The last course created (1973), the Course of Updating of the ESG (CAESG), takes place by correspondence and aims to perform in a more rational and complete way the task of keeping the cadres trained (graduates of the ESG) well updated of the variations in the your knowledge. For this, the graduates are called to the update after five, ten, fifteen years and so on, the completion of one of the regular courses. For the multiplication of representative effects, the Association of Graduates of the Superior School of War (ADESG) has been operating since 1949 in all major Brazilian cities in support of the diffusion of the National Security Doctrine, disseminating concepts and methods in force in ESG through cycles of regular studies to its members[6].

Alfred Stepan[7] (1986) tells us that throughout its existence, ESG had "the period of greatest doctrinal initiative from 1952 to 1956, when most of the ideas took shape. The period of greatest importance was between 1964 and 1967, when many of the members of the most important group of 1952-56 formulated and implemented the directives of the first military government "(p.57). Stepan, incidentally, induces the War College to lose power under the 1964 regime.

In addition, it says that ESG's studies were sent to the Joint Chiefs of Staff and were not necessarily circulated to ministries nor known by them, resulting in less expressiveness, due to the size of the collecting organ and the processor of these studies - the EMFA-being small and not very influential.

On the other hand, it shows that the ESG remained a "key institution" responsible for systematizing, reproducing and disseminating the National Security Doctrine and its relationship with the polis, and which functioned as an authoritative source of the military institution for the expression of its members. It emphasizes the importance of its study, since the system of education and socialization and the legal system based on

---

[5] Law 785, of 20 Aug 1949.

[6] "The State of São Paulo". Introduce yourself on "ESG-30 years influencing national life", from Aug 19, 1979.

[7] STEPAN, Alfred C (1986). *Os militares: da abertura à nova república.* Paz e Terra Editora, Rio de Janeiro.

the National Security Law used official ESG documents as a doctrinal basis (p. 58).

As an internal structure for the training activity, ESG began with the creation of the National, International and Military Affairs Divisions. In 1954, these divisions were replaced by the divisions of Political, Psychosocial, Economic and Military Affairs and an Executive Division to approximate the methodology for the study of national power with the specificity of the treatment of power from the point of view of "expressions", which were studied according to the coherence of the evolution of the ESG doctrine, which is sensitive to the conjuncture conditions. The new configurations of the ESG structure, set up for the adaptation to the conjuncture, demonstrate the flexibility of the planning, observing the rigidity in the use of the method[8].

Details of ESG's initial project and its speech
The organization and the assembly of the military program

The "security & development" proposal needed to be developed in an orchestrated fashion with the participation of modernizing-conservative social agents, considered organic intellectuals[9] of the new bloc in the cold war environment. The political structure formed of the multinational bloc was consolidated in an entrepreneurial intelligentsia. The composition of this select group was, in general: a) directors of multinational corporations; b) managers of private companies, technicians and state executives who were part of the techno-bureaucracy c) a restricted group of Army officers. Such components would represent what René Armand Dreifuss[10] characterized as an association of military and civilians that would make up the "military-techno-bureaucratic arm" of the ideological apparatus of the cold war.

As for the military arm, its modernizing-conservative features were marked by the experiences of officers who went to war in Europe, fighting alongside the US, living a common ideological experience, as well as military. Upon the return of the II WW such officers became members of certain political parties such as the UDN and to a lesser extent the PDC, which ensured representativeness for their innovative ideas.

However, the greatest center representing the new ideas was the ESG, an entity that was notable from the initiative of these officers as agents of its foundation. The following included the group of officers: Golbery de Couto e Silva, Orlando Geisel, Ernesto Geisel, Aurélio de Lyra Tavares, Jurandir Bizarria Mamede, Heitor Almeida Herrera, Edson de Figueiredo, Geraldo de Menezes Cortes, Idálio Sardenberg, Belfort Bethlem, João Bina Machado, Liberato Cunha Friedrich, Ademar de Queiroz, Gustavo Cordeiro de Farias

---

[8] *Op. cit.* Guita Debert shows a synoptic picture on the main milestones of the evolution of the internal and external environment of the ESG in the period 1948/1980.

[9] Gramsci established appropriate theoretical principles for the perception of the process by which the agents of modernizing Brazilian capitalism were formed. He points out that "every social group that comes to exist on the ground originating from an essential function in the world of economic production brings with it, organically, one or more layers of intellectuals that provide homogeneity to the group, as well as the awareness of its own function, not only in the economic field, but also in the social and political fields. The capitalist entrepreneur creates with him the industrial technician, the specialist in political economy, the organizers of a new culture". See HOARE & Geoffrey NOWELL-SMITH. Selections from the prison notebooks of Antonio Gramsci. London, Lawrence & Whishart, 1973, p.5. (Quoted by René Deifuss, *op.cit.*, P.107-108)

[10] DREIFUSS, René Armand. *1964: A Conquista do Estado.* Petrópolis:Vozes,1981,pp.73-75.

and Juarez Távora; some of them had exercised the preponderant role in Brazilian politics.

There was a degree of convergence of affinities of these officers with Lucas Lopes, Roberto Campos, Eugênio Gudin and Octávio Gouveia de Bulhões who shared the ESG classrooms as lecturers. Indeed, there was a well-demarcated space of complicity in the diffusion of developmental ideas, for the military chain of ESG, as Dreifuss points out, "shared with multinational and associated interests both the perspective and the sense of urgency in transforming the rhythm and orientation from the process of growth towards the creation of a capitalist industrial society "(p.78).

There is another component that contributes to intensify the predilection of some of these officers by the bureaucratic-industrial mechanism: the military participation of officers in the private initiative[11] in the 50s and early 60s was seen as the direction of corporate positions or in the corporate control of companies[12], allowed after the 1952 military agreement between Brazil and the United States.

The "Mutual Security Law" in section 516 made it possible to "remove barriers and provide incentives for a steady increase in private enterprise participation in the development of foreign resources and discourage as possible and without interfering in the achievement of the objectives of this law, the practice of monopoly and cartel prevailing in certain countries[13]".

The clauses of the Military Agreement permitted the practice of oligopoly in substitution of state monopoly, diversifying the interference of multinational capital over Brazilian business and facilitating (among which some of the officials mentioned participated in these benefits), in contrast, the use of this industrial potential increased.

In order to set the stage for the first actions of the ESG-Project, marked by the political boil of the 1950s, it is interesting to note what Vanda Aderaldo says about the role of the School. For her, the ESG would be committed to a certain diagnosis of the Brazilian situation and with the purpose of modifying this situation through the right, assumed by the military, to intervene in an inaccurate process of development of the general potential of the Nation as a precondition for the their specific task of ensuring National Security.

The existence of the ESG, therefore, would seem to make no sense if the armed forces were denied the right to intervene in the process of developing the nation's

---

[11] René Dreifuss quotes (p.113) Manwaring, who states that "the occupation by military officers of administrative posts in multinational and associated corporations and the identification of the military with the aims and methods of private enterprises showed, after 1964, a tendency to the consolidation of a military-industrial complex, where industrial, civilian, and military interests associated and sought joint production and where officers of the Armed Forces were employed by private corporations as key men. "See MANWARING, M. The military in Brazilian politics. Doctoral thesis. Illinois, Univ. Of Illinois, 1966.

[12] Some officers and their correlations with the company: General Riograndino Kruel and General James Masson (Eletronica Kruel SA), General Paulo Tasso de Resende (mills Rio-grandenses Samrig SA- Bung & Born group), Brigadeiro Eduardo Gomes (kosmos engenharia SA) , General Edmundo Macedo Soares e Silva (Volkswagen, Mesbla SA, Mercantile Bank of São Paulo, Light SA, Mercedes-Benz), General Euclides de Oliveira Figueiredo (Industries), General Joaquim Ribeiro Monteiro (Coal Carbonos Coloidais, CCC- Wolney Attalla group) Chemicals and Pharmaceuticals Shering SA- Schering Corporation and Assis Chautebriand group), General Moziul Moreira Lima (Máquinas Moreira SA) and Admiral Álvaro Alberto da Motta e Silva (Rupturita SA Explosives- Sociedade Financeira Portuguesa) (Cited by René Dreifuss, op.cit, p.78).

[13] PEREIRA, Osny D. The antinomy of the US-Brazil military agreement. Rio de Janeiro, Brazilian Association of Democratic Jurists, 15 ab. 1963, p.24 (translated from original source).

potential. The experience of the "Charter of Principles" would reveal an unmanifest debate about the limits of the pedagogical proposal of the School. In fact, the objective of ESG, as a military teaching institution, was an instrumental objective (p.84).

The new task of guaranteeing Hemispheric Security, located in the sphere of foreign policy and arising from Brazil's relations with the United States in the post-war period, would require, according to Vanda Aderaldo[14], a kind of formal preparation of the military for a function with political dimensions institutionalized. It demanded, on the other hand, the socialization of civilians in the understanding that this task, given the circumstances of imminent threat of war, should really be the Armed Forces (p.85).

Contradicted in the official discourse we are led to think that in addition to the intention to cover up the nature of his project, clearly shown by Vanda Aderaldo, there was a concern to combine the pedagogy of the process with a political action that was seen by other authors[15].

In this discussion, Myamoto (1981, p.130) develops his analyzes considering that the proposal to become a center of studies "directed in the formation of an elite that looked for an opportunity to rise to the power". For the author, developing the necessary knowledge to exercise the functions of decision or planning of National Security would justify the seriousness of purpose of putting them into practice. In this way, the creation of elite responsible for the National Security policy would be conditioned to the selective mechanism. It is not without cause that individuals occupying high positions or projections are measured until their recruitment, since for Myamoto[16] this criterion would lead to the assisted propagation of the ESG Doctrine for the government practice in the post-64, considering that the function to serve as an intermediary between the people and the State, as many studies elaborated by the ESG, or "a moderating role in the difficult moments of national life", would have been consciously prepared and endowed with a doctrine of national security to exercise effectively the possession of the state apparatus, achieving the goal in 1964, which would reach the maximum period of its influence.

The National War College and the ESG foundation

It is possible to identify from the author's analysis that the intentions of the School congregated to the motivation of segments of society useful to the expansionist movement of military influence. On this conception, let us see what comes as an official discourse:

> (...) inspired in broad lines in its American counterpart, ESG "departed fundamentally" from the US National War College, as an official 1949 document said, given the distinct characteristics of the two countries, and in view of the fact that in Brazil, alongside the problem of preparation for war prevailing in the

---

[14] ADERALDO, Vanda (1978). The School of War: a study of curriculum and programs, mimeo, IUPERJ, Rio de Janeiro, pp. 84-85. The excellence of this synthesis supports the dimension of the ESG efforts by a societal legitimization, which should be mentioned later in this work, when analyzing its axiological body.

[15] MYAMOTO, Shiguenoli (1981). *O pensamento geopolítico Brasileiro (1920-1980)*. Mimeo,USP,São Paulo. Some of the "others" are: Coelho, Edmundo C .; Debert, Guita G.

[16] MYAMOTO,S.,1981, p.131.

United States, there was still the "pressing problem of organizing national life in times of peace"[17].

According to the text, initially ESG is designed in the style of the National War College, founded in 1946. A North American mission is in charge of guiding the implementation of the School. In fair measure, this seems to be one of the factors that have led authors such as Burguess, M. & Wolf, D[18]. (mentioned by Guita Debert, 1986, p. 88) to see ESG, despite the claims of originality made by its organizers, as a reproduction of the American congener.

In a certain way, it would be in practice "the diffusion in Brazil of the doctrines of the American military establishment and of the systematic formulation of the interests (transformed into politics) of the great multinational and associated national businessmen, driving instrumentally a sector of the Brazilian Armed Forces" (p.16). On this "claim," General Fragoso[19] goes on to say that a small group of officers were, before the commission that founded the School, to the US to obtain their establishment standards.

Limiting the role of the United States to the advisory services for the assembly of the Brazilian School[20], the aim is to increase the reason for Slavic originality from the "pains of childbirth", intentionally seeking to escape criticism from the intelligentsia of society. In this way, the official discourse of the School is developed in order to emphasize its independence and originality in relation to the counterparts of other countries. In Debert's idea[21], such originality would be both in the way in which the School is organized-work is developed with full-time trainees for ten months, ESG, unlike the American School, is attended by civilians and the latter, as opposed to what is happening in the English congener, are not only high officials of the State, but also in relation to the theoretical thought developed in its interior, as for example, with regard to the "modern" concept of Security and its relation with the development.

The close relationship between Security and Development, which was only developed in 1968 by Robert MacNamara in the foreword to the book "Security and Development", was present at the School since its formation, the first of the principles guiding the creation of ESG.

---

[17] Article of the Army General Augusto Fragoso, commander of the ESG of 1967/1971 published in the "State of São Paulo"newspaper on August19, 1979.

[18] BURGUESS, Mike & Wolf, Daniel. (1980). *Brasil: o conceito de Poder na Escola Superior de Guerra*, in Revista de Cultura Vozes, ano 75, vol.LXXIV, n 5,jun/jul.Rio de Janeiro.

[19] At the forefront of the preparatory work for the implementation of the ESG, General César Obino, Head of the EMFA, who, with a small group of officers, went to the United States in 1948, before the Cordeiro Commission, to study the organization of the National War College, founded two years earlier. The result of this visit was the signing of a contract with the US of a US military mission composed of three senior officers (one from each force) to collaborate in the ESG institution.

[20] ESG is called "Escola", coming directly from Portuguese. Sometimes, in keeping with this tradition, I will use the word School to designate it, restraining the political-pegagogical character in preaching the necessary fundamentals of security and defense necessary for Brazilian society.

[21] *Op cit.*,p.89. The analysis is exactly that of the author.

The originality of the ESG's proposal as the original military policy

Debert[22] goes on to cite how such originality also refers to the differences between American and Brazilian society, in the view of the School, commenting on how there is a departure. The latter, acting in a more developed environment in which the educational system which formed the elites was charged with instilling a method of work and solving general problems already enshrined in national life, would not need to re-touch this point would clearly guide the expansion of the field of knowledge and its immediate application in war.

The proposed School in Brazil would find a different environment: in Brazil the problem of preparation for war is so permanent. For her, Brazil is still struggling to solve the problem of national life in times of peace; on the other hand, recognizes that our backwardness is mainly motivated by the defect of the educational system that empowers elites with general knowledge, but does not arm them with resources to objectively and harmoniously solve the problems of national life. ESG would therefore aim to fill this gap and, in addition, to provide knowledge about war preparation and the conduct of combined operations (p.89) in the study of national and international problems.

Another approach, however, considers that the existence of the School, in partnership with the US military, was essentially to materialize the hemispheric security[23] proposal, which coincided with the National Security vision for the moment. In a sense, the environment of dichotomous clashes caused by ideological rivalries between the Christian West and the Communist East would tend to privilege Development Security. It is at this point that Debert believes in the distancing of the original version of the Americanized ESG, since soon the School adopts the binomial Security & Development like motto.

To this extent, Debert cites Aderaldo's view (1978, pp. 80-81) that points to the creation of the ESG under the need to make explicit a project for Brazil originating from the Armed Forces, makes the relation that the reform of Benjamin Constant would correspond to an imperative referred only to the context of professional training, and the Góes Monteiro Statute, in the broader context of the Army organization, as a national institution within the power structure would have originated from the demands of the conflicts and alliances that emerged in the international scenario from the Second World War. The participation of the Brazilian Army in this war, according to the author, would have been its first experience of international relations, as an organization.

From then on, the elite became aware of its strategic importance in conducting the negotiations and alliances that made up the framework of the Cold War. Historically, the chain of relations from which the organizational limits of the armed institution were established would be closed. Thus, the remaining issue was to situate the Brazilian Army within the framework of international political relations that was taking shape.

The independence and evolution of the Army leading to ESG

In this same line of study of the organizational path, it is important to report the

---

[22] ESG, T1-80,1980, pp.29-30.
[23] CAMARGO, Sonia. (s/d). *Militares e Geopolítica no Brasil*, mimeo, PUC- Rio de Janeiro.

approach of Edmundo Campos Coelho[24] that shows the insufficiency of the analyzes based on an instrumental conception of the Armed Forces, i. e., the types of considerations that restrict themselves to showing the Armed Forces as merely an instrument for the achievement of the objectives of the ruling classes, which have the acute expression in the works of Nelson Werneck Sodré or the interests of the Brazilian middle classes, as it appears in Hélio Jaguaribe[25]. Coelho points out that ESG, as the center of the National Security Doctrine, is the result of an evolutionary process of the Armed Forces as an institution.

The origin of this process would be located in the coming of the French Mission to Brazil, in a proposal for the formation of a doctrine for the Army. The decade of the lieutenants would be characterized by insurgency manifestations against the lack of professionalization of senior officers committed to the corrupt oligarchic structure. To that extent, the revolution of 1930 would not only have neutralized the current of the lieutenants, but would have also abandoned the oldest and incompetent officers (in the professionalized environment), allowing the intermediate generations a great upward benefit.

From this wing of officers, Coelho highlights Góes Monteiro as one of the main drafters of a coherent and global conception of relations between the Army and society. For Coelho, this conception coincides with the National Security Doctrine elaborated by the intelligence of ESG, only reworked according to another conjuncture (1976, p. 105). On the professional profile of Goés Monteiro[26], Coelho, E. C., makes an interesting description of his profile, revealing that he developed a curious trajectory, from his entry in the ranks of the Army. However, some occurrences throughout his military life would have qualified him as a man prepared to engender the changes that the military institution needed[27]. The condition of his unique influence can be

---

[24] COELHO,E.C., (1976). *Em busca de identidade: o Exército e a Política na sociedade brasileira.* Forense Universitária, Rio de Janeiro.

[25] SODRÉ, N.W., (1968).*História Militar do Brasil.* Civilização Brasileira, Rio de Janeiro.

JAGUARIBE,H., (1969). *Desenvolvimento Econômico e Desenvolvimento Político.* Paz e Terra, Rio de Janeiro.

[26] Op.cit. Edmundo (1976: 98-99) cites the personal profile of Góes Monteiro, extracted from the impression of the then Lieutenant Argemiro of Assis Brasil, " O Gal. Góes e dois problemas nacionais", in Bertholdo Klinger, Euclydes Figueiredo, Othelo Franco, José Lobo e Argemiro de Assis Brasil, *Nós e a Ditadura*, pp.154-155:endowed with great insight, insinuating and of fine intelligence, the General Góes Monteiro knows how to take the occasion by the hair, coldly mask his true intentions with ingenious abstractions, satisfying, more often than not, exclusively, his nature of political exhibitionism. He does not fear prejudices; it firmly and cautiously relies on all available resources. Unite enemies to swallow them. It circumvents events and transposes obstacles into jumps. Ally one enemy for the defeat of the other. Your personal friends are function of the resources that can provide you in the accomplishment of your inflexible goals. Take advantage of the more clumsy personalities. In all men you find qualities to be put into service. The traitor, the energetic man, the spy, the scoundrel, the brave, the man of character, etc.-all this is good merchandise in the hands of this great manufactor. No one finds any clear resistance. You lose here, to win later. It apparently follows the entourage's inflows. Always disdain her. "

[27] Pedro Aurélio de Góes Monteiro. Born in the State of Alagoas, he was of humble origin and, for that reason, chose the military career less for vocation than for simple employment. At the age of 14 he had joined the Military School and at the age of 20 had been a candidate for the officer. at a time when military education was focused on the physical and mathematical sciences, the young officer stood out in the strictly military disciplines. He could not finish the Artillery courses, weapon of his own. Transferred to the Cavalry, it caused an unflattering impression on the French instructors. He was, however, the first student in his class and then appointed assistant professor. He made an obscure career, almost always in minor

materialized in the absence of clichés and commonplaces that are normally used by military chiefs to conceal differences and internal cleavages or to handle difficulties within the military spirit. Coelho comments that Goes made no allusions to the unshakable cohesion, glorious past, self-denial of the chiefs, cult of discipline or any other formula of style. On the contrary, its perception of facts and the historical interpretation of relations between the Army and society are essentially critical and realistic (1976, p.100).

Some of his ideas, fundamental to the military doctrine of the Army and the New State, provided an unprecedented acceleration in this perspective: "(...) I have always felt that we live in a country that, despite appearances to the contrary, has a kind of repulsed by the military spirit, and since colonial times, what has prevailed in military soi disant organizations is the militia or praetorian spirit and not the true spirit of the soldier" (p.101).

Army policies instead of army politics

In this case, in order to reinforce the positive image of the military institution, Góes explains that the problem of national defense posed as aggravated by the class struggle preached at that moment would have the Army, in its view, to be an essentially political body, since all aspects of politics affect doctrine and the potential for war (p.103).

Goes continues with the consideration that could synthesize the proposal for the renewal of the Army as an entity qualified to discuss national problems, with consequences for Brazilian politics in the years to come, since, based on the premise of an essentially political Army, it encourages the creation of a collective conscience favorable to an Army policy and not to an army policy (pp.104-105), set at the core of society that would lack the organizational principle of the Armed Forces, that is, a militarization of society, paradoxically without having the spirit militaristic.

The foregoing demonstrates what would be the embryonic proposition for the National Security Doctrine already commented on as the preferential approach of Coelho (p.105). He himself relates the military doctrine to the "Estado Novo"(1937-45) with the creation of the ESG that would, in fact, extend the scope to him. "Thus, the Security & Development formula on which the philosophy of the post-1964 revolutionary governments is based is, in essence, a more sophisticated, systematized and updated version of the idea developed by Góes Monteiro that national defense is, "at the same time, factor and result of a national development policy that to be

---

functions of General Staff, until the beginning of the revolutionary movement of 1930. The military leadership of this movement had been reserved for Luis Carlos Prestes until his definitive conversion to Marxism became evident. There is evidence that the then Lieutenant Colonel Góes Monteiro was only decided by the revolutionary action when the articulation of the movement was already advanced. In order to accept military leadership, it imposed conditions which were initially unacceptable, that is to say, personal and indivisible command in everything that concerns purely military operations. He had political culture superior to the average of the officers of his generation, acquired by effort of selfdidatism. He was the main inspirer and articulator of the Estado Novo and strong man of the regime. Without being esteemed within the Army, his prestige was undeniable. What we will call military doctrine and politics of the time was the intellectual work of this man, of whom it was said, significantly, that "he was already general since lieutenant".

effective presupposes as a necessary condition an overall strategy of rigidly restraining the struggling political forces and social discipline". None of the factions in which the Army eventually divided up after the 1930s questioned such conceptions at any time. Whatever their personal political attitudes, the Brazilian military has always disdained the existing political processes, the incapacity and personality of the civil elites and the social indiscipline of the citizen."(1976, p. 114)

As a result of the unanimous assertion made by the military public, it seems plausible to choose a single establishment to centralize the Armed Forces' aspirations for its development, under the aegis of Security. Góes Monteiro[28] would have anticipated this when he characterized the Army and the Navy as truly national institutions, in which the other "forces of nationality" would be mirrored.

The ESG as an expression of the superiority of the military institution over civilians in the great Brazilian project

The approach of Oliveira, E.R.[29], comments on how this privileged Brazilian Armed Forces's self-view that leads to the National Security Doctrine (DSN) tends to discriminate against other institutions, opening spaces for greater military occupation of space in the national and international scenario, while at the same time ideologically "closing" the socializing life, which is almost always present in the crisis of the state of bourgeois domination (pp. 25-26).

According to Burguess, M. & Wolf, D.[30], the inability of Brazilian elites to adequately interpret and apply the aspirations of the people channels fundamental causes of the crisis and Brazilian problems. With the ESG doctrine, comes a new possibility of solving the national problem, according to the objective of the military institution. This discussion would follow from the point of view of the ESG: "if on the one hand the Brazilian people are declared historically" prodigal (unable to decide for themselves their own destiny), on the other hand and as a consequence of the difficulties of the so-called historical-cultural method, elites have not always been able to correctly interpret and express the aspirations of the people, nor have they been able to discard their particular interests so as to be able to express the true interests of the people. In this fact lies one of the fundamental causes of the crisis and the Brazilian problems. Brazilian society has, however, an element that fulfills the essential requirements of a real elite: the military, since they "have power only with the country, follow clear principles of nationalism, represent more than any popular forces, and as a qualification of the rhetoric the people in government "(TI 123, 1972, ESG, p.52, *op.cit*).

This vision of being, originating from ESG itself that military elites would be able to lead the country politically, comes from this disbelief that there was a national elite capable of leading national development. The sense of the School is precisely to prepare it, promoting the union between civilians and military, according to Guita

---

[28] GOES M., Pedro Aurélio. *A Revolução de 30 e a Finalidade Política do Exército*. Rio de Janeiro: Adersen Editores, pp.156-157.

[29] OLIVEIRA, Eliézer Rizzo (1976). *As Forças Armadas: política e ideologia no Brasil (1964-1969)*. Vozes, Petrópolis.

[30] *Op cit.*, p.26.

Debert (1986, p.213) claims to see in all their speeches. The author comments that this fact allows a positive reference to be made at all times to the originality of the School, already mentioned, in relation to its counterparts in the world. To say, therefore, that it is a question of giving a new role only to the military, would be to reduce the pure phraseology not only the speeches, but also the practice itself that precisely because of the presence of civilians differs from other schools of the same gender. In fact, civilians, even under the military initiative, from the beginning were a fundamental part of the ESG Project.

Alfred Stepan[31], implying the military necessity to express a new ideology for the period, says that the School went on to elaborate studies of a political-economic-social nature, in the presence of distinguished lecturers and students (what is perhaps the segmentation of the elite criticized by the Brazilian left), always with the motivation of the use of the business nature for the task of maintaining National Security (1975, pp. 127-129). This fact, besides the originality intended, would legitimize the complicity of the national bourgeoisie with the Project, guaranteeing the perpetuation and making possible the results, under the aegis of development, multiplied in the Brazilian policy.

ESG, its discourse and its conjunction with Brazilian authoritarian thinking
   The doctrine of ESG in its inspiring sources: positivism

Myamoto (1995, p. 80) writes that the Doctrine of National Security includes the influence of the thought of Alberto Torres, Oliveira Viana, Auguste Comte and Góes Monteiro, who would have been amalgamated. Thus, it points to important parts to be analyzed in the whole ideological body of the School. Confronting the production of the ESG and its inspiring sources, it seems clear that authoritarianism is present in all. Góes Monteiro, as shown, motivated the change of doctrinal patterns of the Armed Forces, starting from a period of experimentation in the regime of force of the New-State[32].

It is necessary to verify how authoritarian thinkers like Alberto Torres and Oliveira Viana gain space in the conception of the School. Eliézer Rizzo de Oliveira confirms that "the thinking of Alberto Torres and Oliveira Viana weighed considerably on the central conceptions of the ESG that, due to its vision of the Brazilian process, had to feed on other sources and other motivations in the situation itself international"[33]. It is also necessary to consider the Auguste Comte's reflex in the articulation of its methodology and this is the extension of the own educational[34] principles for the official of the Army.

---

[31] STEPAN, Alfred. *Os Militares na Política*. Rio de Janeiro: Arte Nova,1975.

[32] DINIZ, Eli (1991). The New State: structure of power and class relations, in HGCB, vol.III-Society and Politics (1930-1964), Bertrand Brazil Editora S.A, Rio de Janeiro, p.118. He comments on gradual independence and a progressive increase in the power of the army and its role with society after the neutralization of the tenentist faction and says that "... if this role cannot be reduced to a simple instrument of the power from Getulio Vargas, in the so much so that the Army would assert itself as an organization precisely in pursuit of its own objectives, questioning the validity of the use of the military corporation by the political factions in their internal disputes, finally rebelling against the subordination of the Army to the interests of the party struggle, on the other hand, Estado Novo would not be a military dictatorship. "

[33] OLIVEIRA, Eliézer Rizzo. *Militares : pensamento e ação política*. Papirus Editora, Campinas, SP, p.62.

Let us see how the ESG thinks about the ideas it has appropriated from authoritarian thinkers. ESG, represented by one of members of permanent body[35] declares that the thoughts of Alberto Torres and Oliveira Viana are in their headquarters, but criticizes the association with integralism. In addition, he obviously contradicts himself when he says that Michel Schooyans's book, "Destin du Brésil" (1973), which pointed to the positivism of the beginning of the Republic with its "Order and Progress" as the predecessor of Security & Development, does not express reality of ESG thinking.

On the other hand, it makes clear that in its doctrine are the "national objectives" well demarcated by the theory of Oliveira Viana. The political pedagogy for the reform of the institutions as there is the support of a resistance in the official discourse on the non positivist bases of the Doctrine of the War College, one thinks of a purposive escapade of the positivist nature for the ESG, considering that there was a rivalry of intentions between "cientificistas" and "professionalistas" throughout History of the Education of the Army, according to Jehovah Mota (See 1998, p. 175).

Celso Castro then shows that scientism permeates the military thinking of the young officers of the late Empire (and who will be the army generals of the 1930s), bringing the hassle of his presence to the wing of the military corporation focused on professionalization of the Army as a way of its rapid evolution, if represented by ESG. In Castro's description, Auguste Comte's positivism (1798-1857) could be synthesized in three basic themes. First, a philosophy of history based on the "law of the three states."

According to this law, the human spirit (and with it all the sciences) would pass through three phases: theological, metaphysical and positive. In the theological phase,

---

[34] MOTTA, Jehovah (1998). *Formação do Oficial do Exército:currículos e regimes na Academia Militar, 1810-1944.* Biblioteca do Exército Editora, Rio de Janeiro. Regarding the discussion of the relationship between Auguste Comte's influence on Brazilian military education, although the official discourse of the ESG disagrees with its connection, observe what the author says: ... "The position of Benjamin Constant puts us, once again, in view of the crucial problem of determining what quantum of general culture is necessary for the training of the Army officer. If the curriculum must coexist elements of two categories, the general, basic, scientific, and professional knowledge, linked to the routine of military matters, can only be structured properly by those who have a fair idea of the dosage to be assigned to each of them. This dosage-this is the great question always raised and never resolved by the Academy in more than one hundred years of life. Two theses have always faced, in this century and a half of curricular lucubrations: that of "culturalists", or "scientisticians", who overvalued general, scientific studies, improperly called theoretical studies, and "professionalists" for whom know eminently application and directly functional. It is evident that the right solution will be to flee from any extreme position, for the benefit of one that avoids, at the same time, the uniformed doctor. but ignorant of military processualism, and the empty official of general scientific knowledge, a kind of agaly-petty officer, master of simple elementary skills, incapable of seeing causes, accompanying evolutions and preparing for progress "(175).

[35] Article written by Ubiratan de Macedo, at that time belonging to the permanent body of ESG, having been filled in the Division of research and doctrine. The article was transcribed by "Jornal do Brasil" on August 19, 1979, on the occasion of the 30th anniversary of ESG, under the title: ESG Doctrine comes from Vianna and Alberto Torres (Translation). The attempt to discharacterize the influence of the Comteano thought in the ESG is not able to subsist by the reinforcement given to the method. The basic ESG manual (1993: 30) talks about several concepts interrelated with the "binomial" Security & Development. The origin of these concepts is hidden, but contradicts itself therefore "as to the method, the School was worth of the teachings of Descartes, following, in fact, a tradition of our military schools". Now, this methodology coincides with positivism, as explained.

man tries to explain nature through belief in spirits and supernatural beings. In this state, imagination would play a greater role than observation of phenomena. Absolute confidence in the authority of supernatural beings would lead, on the one hand, to social cohesion; on the other, on the political level, to the monarchy founded on militarism. The metaphysical state would use abstract argument instead of imagination. With this, the supernatural will is replaced by natural ideas or forces, breaking with the theological notion of the absolute subordination of Nature and man to the supernatural sphere. At the political level, jurists take the place of kings, starting with the notion of contract, and the state is no longer based on a divine origin, but on popular sovereignty. In the positive state, the place of Comte's philosophy of history, imagination and argument are subordinated to observation.

We begin to seek to understand no more the intimate nature of things, but their laws, constant relations between observable phenomena. Filled with a tradition that passes through Bacon, Galileo, and Descartes, Comte demonstrates blind faith in the progress and role of science as a guide to social and personal life, for knowledge of natural and social laws would make it possible to predict the future.

The great development of technology in the positive state would lead to the industrial-industrial regime in the sense of the exploration of nature by man-with the substitution of the power of jurists for that of scientists and industrialists and the universal conception of humanity. The second basic theme of Comte's philosophy would be to propose a classification of the sciences, a scale which would begin with the one whose object is the most simple and indeterminate, allowing a consequent greater degree of generality, inversely, the most complex and specific: mathematics, astronomy, physics, chemistry, biology and sociology.

Sociology would allow the generalization of knowledge, relating it to the idea of humanity. In the composition of sociology there would be a "social static", which would study the constant conditions of society (order), and a "social dynamics", which studies the laws of its development (progress). The third basic theme of comtean philosophy, according to Castro's exposition, is the reform of institutions, carried out by the new scientific-industrial elite.

This would not be done through a revolution, but through the intellectual reform of man (1995, pp. 64-65). The way Celso Castro[36] describes the positivist view demonstrates the reinforcement of this ideology on the themes of "order and progress" in political action, in addition to being a mere pedagogical proposal of emphasis in the natural sciences. The degree of abstraction that Benjamin Constant[37], Comte's adept at the end of the Empire, proposed to be gradually worked on in the curriculum of the

---

[36] CASTRO, Celso (1995). *Os Militares e a República: um estudo sobre cultura e ação política.* Jorge Zahar Editora, Rio de Janeiro, pp.63-64.

[37] The reference is in Jehovah Mota, *A Formação do Oficial do Exército*, p.155, op. cit. Cândido Mariano da Silva Rondon said that "Benjamin Constant operated the almost superhuman prodigy of transfiguring his chair of Algebraic Geometry on an altar raised to the purest idealization of the Homeland. In fact, this prodigy has its easy explanation: refusing to dwell on the mere exposition of curricular matter, on the contrary, rising to philosophical considerations about sciences, and of these on sociology, Benjamin expressed the needs of a rising social stratum and in search of new conceptual instruments capable of opening the way to social and political action. He was expressive of the yearnings of the middle class that, at the influx of the transformations of the economic structure, gradually became opulent and prepared for the disputes of the political scene. He and his audience were complete, lived for one another, merged into one exaltation: the search for the changes they idealized and foreseen ... ".

Military School, would suggest the insertion of Sociology as a foundation for the exercise of military leadership. Such leadership, if allied to Comte's ideas for a technicalism capable of leading to the "industrial regime" and the consequent "substitution of jurists for industrialists", could formulate something similar to the phenomenon of the ESG, although the official discourse purposely, reply to this. Moreover, the third basic theme of comtean philosophy, the reform of institutions, through a "new scientific-industrial and technological elite," also shows an affinity with the School's ideology.

Thus, projecting itself into the future, Dreyfuss (1981, p.71) alludes to an association of military and civilians, via ESG, that would make up the military-techno-bureaucratic arm of the ideological apparatus of the cold war and established in its post- 64.

Organicism and the Military Elite in the ESG's Doctrine

Eliézer Rizzo de Oliveira (1987, p. 71) explores the subject when he explains that this elite is chosen by the military elite and later prepared for the exercise of power, showing how the theoretical arrangement supported by Oliveira Viana and Alberto Torres in the conception of egoism of the elites (for political direction) and the unpreparedness of the masses (for political participation).

Thus, he speaks of the "inability" of these two social groups generically designed to organize the Nation, as well as the unpreparedness of the social body for any major historical task. Such a lack of preparation would be manifest through the lack of methods of investigation of social reality (hence the Doctrine proposal as a method of global inquiry that goes beyond the custom of "opinions" to particular problems of government"), in prejudice to planning, lack of critical capacity of political institutions. On the other hand, Eliezer says that the degree of extension, penetration, organization and integration of the military apparatus at the level of national power contrasts with the superficial implementation of professional parties and associations.

However, the most important part of the analysis is to understand that the military receive training that identifies them as part of the elites destined to direct the destinies of the country. According to him, there are numerous examples of this in Brazilian military history, such as discouraging the coexistence of cadets from the Realengo Military School with the simple residents of that Rio suburb or mechanisms that make the official experience distant from the conditions previously dictated by the class which originated.

Like their colleagues in the Empire, the military that created the ESG would have developed the notion that, as members of the elite, it would be up to them to teach these elite to run the country. For if civil elites often put their private interests above any social consideration, the military, on the contrary, would have all the moral qualifications and political conditions to fight for the common good (which they would already represent in the state). These militaries, in Eliezer's approach, are conceived as the only authentic elite, to a choice of the sectors of the civil elites to be articulated in the effort of a constitution of the ruling elite. The military would assume this political-pedagogic way.

In another approach, analyzing the way in which state and change are seen in

Brazilian authoritarian thinking, Bolívar Lamounier (1977, p.362) makes some considerations about the structure of the State Ideology, which compels us to compare them with the placements made by ESG. This author shows that the proto-fascist ideologies that dominated European thought were not simply transplanted to Brazil, but their assimilation took place in a very particular way by Brazilian thought.

Here there would have been an accentuation of the positivist element and the conservative aspects of the organicist language; that is, the organicist metaphor is used to express a conservative view of the change that is intended to trigger, emphasizing the durability of the past in the present, the perception of growth and change, as the development of an internal principle contained in the origin, the indispensable maturation of the body before the implementation of institutional reforms or grafts. Strong state power would be necessary, not only to eradicate the evils of the past, whose inertial force can only be overcome by energetic surgery, but also to keep under control the very process of change, ensuring the survival of the usable.

The appropriation of organicist logic by ESG is also seen by Eliézer Rizzo de Oliveira when he comments that the world view of the Doctrine of National Security includes a legal-administrative view of the State, conceived as an organism and instrument of power; "an organicist and functional view of society, where the parties necessarily collaborate for the integration and survival of the whole "(1987, p.73).

Alberto Torres and his Modern Politics

The need for strong state power of authoritarian thought seems to be a formula for the reshaping of national politics. Alberto Torres (1933) discusses this condition, considering that one of the great errors of social development would have consisted precisely in the emancipation and autonomy of the special branches of knowledge, promoting research and initiating reforms, the influx of stimuli and particular ends. To the policy, the initial and global art of man's life in society in the physical environment, it would henceforth be the task of enriching all other practical arts, in order to indicate to them the opportunities and means of action, making every progress in the proper place and in its time, "avoiding the precipitations and inversions of social development, which, with the appearance of progress, would represent only abortions or leaps of evolution" (Cf. p.225).

Torres, in his speech, goes on to state that "the politics of a nation is an organic policy, which is to say: a policy of harmony, of harmony of equilibrium", in the same way as presented as an ideology of ESG thinking seen by Eliézer Rizzo de Oliveira, as shown. Alberto Torres, pointing to the difficulties of the masses (characterized as the lowest layer of society that does not have the precise means to form a people) would receive the synthesis of the result of the political action that would lead it in a progressive, convergent and harmonious way that means a "superorganic synergy of political forces" (1933, pp. 238-239).

On the condition of the country's defense says that the reasons for the security of the nation should not be attached to the military role, but "that our best defense - one could almost say the only one - is that of avoiding the motives or, if you will, the pretexts of conflict. And this can only be achieved with an austere reorganization of the country, in a regime of strict legality, severe and zealous administration "(p.302).

In this development of Torres it is possible to identify the critique of federalism that brings autonomy, but also the dissolution of the regime, whereas centralization would tend, through austere political action, to a formula of security with development, well compatible with that developed by ESG.

The idea of re-education of the elites of Oliveira Viana and the Armed Forces

In another authoritarian thinker, Oliveira Viana[38], in his book The twilight of the Empire, there is the comment that a little more patriotism of civilian politicians could rule out the greater interference of the military in party politics (1959: 136).

Considering this, the author reveals interesting distinctive aspects about the military's behavior in relation to the civilian, emphasizing the probable pretension of the Brazilian officers to consider themselves the elite.

For him, there would be a radical incompatibility between the psychology of the military and the principles, according to which the activities of the parties in our country are developed. Such radical incompatibility would make political struggles, in which military appearances, a source of fearful friction. In this sense, the military would have, by effect, by education and duty, the very living sentiment of his personal honor, the dignity of his uniform and his gallons: the very condition of a warrior in perspective, a man destined to a mission of bravery, would perfectly justify this special mentality. The soldier would have to be absolutely uncompromising about his professional honor, which is bravery. In civilian life, this honor would end up having a secondary importance and the failure to show at that point the gold belt of the champions would never have been a sensuous snub for a civilian. The military, on the contrary, would have to move away from his weapon-like personality, the slight suspicion of fear or the lack of fearlessness. It is therefore extremely sensitive to offenses. Hence, it is always here an easily explosive element when it penetrates or comes into contact with the electrified atmosphere of civil strife (pp. 136-137).

With another work, "Problems of Organization and Problems of Direction," Oliveira Viana[39] reflects his proposal for the development of the Brazilian State, from his view of preeminence of authority over freedom, not due to "strange theories", but fruit the observation of the Brazilian people in their studies of Brazil and its political history (1974, p. 100). On the Brazilian people, he specifies that the problems of the postwar period (II WW) would suggest the need for leading elites of a new type, provided with a mentality different from the dominant mentality; "elites who, however, would need to be created, since this would be their own national survival" (p. 131). Therefore, it has the proposal of reeducation of the elites, thus described:

"In relation to our people, it is a whole new policy that we have to conceive,

---

[38] VIANA, Oliveira (1959). *O Ocaso do* Império. José Olympio Editora, 3 Edição, Rio de Janeiro. Indeed, this discussion already begun on the assumption of the Brazilian officer of his competence to exercise political power, due to his austere profile that is reinforced by an authoritarian thinker, extols his virtues as a modernizing agent, capable of making change be conservative. This, in my view, appears with an opening for the ESG Project.

[39] VIANA, Oliveira (1974). *Problemas de Organização e Problemas de Direção: o povo e o governo*. Record Editora, 2 edição, Rio de Janeiro.

organize and systematize, in order to eliminate any system of ideas or prejudices that embark on adaptation of our people to the new conditions of the international environment in which we live". Since it was not possible to isolate itself from this environment, being condemned to live in it, there was only one possible solution to the problem of its existence and survival: "it is adapt to this environment; without sacrificing, of course, our independence and the peculiarities of our personality" (p.132). He goes on to describe that the educational problem is, in the end, to conform the individual to certain ends for the "active adaptation" to the environment which would occur through re-education. Yes, exactly this: re-education of ruling elites. "I say elites and not masses, because I am one of those who believe that people are worth the moral and intellectual value of their ruling classes and that nations are saved or perished by the capacity or incapacity of their elites". Right or wrong, good or evil, "this is the new spirit of the times, whose affective force, whose moral determinism the whole Modern State is dependent on and whose fate we cannot escape" (pp.131-134).

I believe although marked by such interventions of intellectuals concerned with Brazilian genuineness, the "cold war" environment was responsible for reinforcing the suggestions on the policy of doctrinal formulation focused on Security and Defense, and the "displacement of the center of gravity of the individual to the group (the nation)" benefits the qualification of the Armed Forces as an agent of the re-education process, since it points to the Armed Forces as one "centers of education of the man in this sense", and according to Viana (pp. 27-28).

2 . ESG AND THE CURRENTS OF BRAZILIAN MILITARY THINKING

The doctrine of ESG

Doctrinal Foundations of ESG

The pretension to identify part of the discussions about the doctrine of the School in the version of the own or in the version of several researchers already runs the risk of erroneous generalizations, due to the difficulties of access to reliable sources, concealed for political reasons. In fact, often the doctrine of the ESG is the National Security Doctrine itself (DSN) widely used during the regime of force and based on principles of hemispheric security and perfectly adequate for the expansion of the Military Institution, as already discussed.

However, it is sometimes perceived as a nuisance of military agents to characterize the doctrine of the School as a precursor or in its identity with it. In order to try to point out the problem, the position of President Humberto de Alencar Castelo Branco[40] was chosen first in the inaugural class of the Superior School of War (ESG), on March 13, 1967. Castillo opens his speech emphasizing the theme chosen for the lesson "Security & Development is a dominant subject in your program, doctrinal in your studies and now integrated in its essence, in the new Brazilian Constitution and in modern laws".

In these initial words, Castelo Branco[41] reveals how the subject would be intensely debated and explored throughout the School year for being "dominant" and "doctrinal". In addition, its insertion in the constitutional text suggests its publicity, possibility offered to the newspaper that did this transcription. Castelo Branco then

---

[40] Castelo Branco was a student and member of the Permanent School Corps. All the reconstitution of the inaugural class comes under the printed form of the newspaper O Globo, on Mar 14, 1967, p.12, with the title: "Castelo Branco exposes new concept of security: global defense". This apparition would have been one of the earliest explanations of the 'Binomial Safety & Development' vision for society, although the School was already created in this vision (1949 onwards).

[41] *Ibidem*

passes on his perception of national security, pointing out that the notion of national security is more comprehensive, encompassing the global defense of institutions and therefore incorporating psychosocial aspects, preservation of international political stability and development. In addition, its concept of security, much more explicitly than that of defense, would take into account internal aggression embodied in ideological infiltration and subversion, even in guerrilla movements, more likely forms of conflict than external aggression in that Cold War.

The overcoming of the understanding of security as a defense, materialized by protection from ostensive attacks by alien nations in conventional warfare, was on the balance sheet of the ideological combat of the Cold War. Subversion and disorder should be seen as the internal aggressions of an infiltrating external enemy in national life. Hence, see the protection of institutions as frameworks of security policy. In any case, it has already been explained that the military vocation for this necessary institutional transformation is well before this period.

Castelo Branco in his exposition[42] then proceeds by making the relationships between development and security which in turn, he understands as connected by a relationship of mutual chance. On one side, true security would presuppose a process of economic-social development; economic, because military power would also be essentially conditioned to the industrial and technological base of the country. Social, because even a satisfactory economic development, if accompanied by excessive concentration of income and increasing social gap, would generate tensions and struggles that would impede the good practice of the institutions and would end up jeopardizing the own economic development and the security of the regime. On the other hand, economic and social development would lead to a minimum of security and stability of institutions.

In fact, the good practice of institutions (my emphasis) could be ensured by a modernization of their structures for results compatible with the development associated with security. As already explained, the proposal of the military institution tending to the re-education of elites would allow the Armed Forces as entities with assured institutional stability, to serve as a model for the political action program proposed by Castelo Branco.

In addition, the disbelief of civilian competence for this modernization of institutions, so seen by the military throughout their interventions in the course of Brazilian history, would reinforce such a hypothesis already seen and quoted by authoritarian thinkers. Castelo Branco[43] also continues to show its reasons for the National Security Doctrine, mobilizing to allege that doctrine, as well as the concept of strategy, does not constitute a rigid body of principles and that it bears ideological, technological and economic influences.

The doctrinal influence is exemplified by him by territorial expansionism, which would have led to the construction of "great empires, which were deemed possessed of a civilizing mission; by ideological expansionism, characteristic of Marxist systems; or by isolationism, as occurred at certain stages of American history." In the Brazilian case, the long Brazilian pacifist tradition would have led us to an essentially defensive doctrine. The option that presents us is between a concept of security eminently

---

[42] *Ibidem*

[43] *Ibidem*

nation which it would see as ineffective in the modern world and among the schemes of associative defense, where we would think in terms of continental security. The doctrine of national security would vary according to technological influences. In the restricted field of military defense, radical transformations would open up several doors to the more developed and technically advanced industrial economy. He says "It is no wonder, then, that in a short space of time a number of doctrines have appeared; the doctrine of final deterrence, in which a contraction of conventional weapons is admitted, and that of concentrating economic and technical resources on nuclear weapons".

The passive defense formula was not worth the size of the total war waged between the east-west blocs. What would be the Brazilian alignment trend? Geographic proximity would make it easier to approach the US, in addition to its pressures to compel Brazil to do so.

In any case, Castelo does not seem to consider much the expansionist nature of US State Department policy. Referring only to moments of his "isolationism", in relation to Soviet "expansionism" he privileges one another, in a frank declaration of the basis that he believes can lead to large-scale military conflicts, in short: a total and totalizing war of non conventional armaments (guerrilla, terrorism, psychological warfare and so on).

On this view, Castelo Branco[44] makes considerations that the relation of nuclear capacity between the two superpowers, US and USSR, would lead to a severe impasse, since the direct confrontation would result in irreparable damage to the planet. This technical observation and the sense of responsibility exhibited by the two powers, aggravated by the dramatic and catastrophic consequences of the use of their nuclear power, would render nuclear conflict increasingly unlikely, thus rehabilitating conventional forces, unique to the type of remaining conflict, constituted by indirect confrontations, through the so-called liberation wars or revolutionary wars, insurrection, counterinsurgency and even guerrilla movements.

Thus, the doctrine of "final deterrence" would be replaced in Castelo Branco's approach with the "flexible response", which requires a combination of nuclear weapons and conventional weapons, otherwise the superpowers would not have two extreme hypotheses: the hecatomb or the inertia. Another example that would give of the technological influences on the doctrine of security is the one of the debate in the Cold War between the two great nuclear powers; debate between those who proposed concentrating efforts on the increase and diversification of attack missiles and those who proposed huge investments in anti-missile defense systems.

Concerning the contradictions that the Cold War brings to the relationship between economic and technological development and military power, Castelo Branco cites the example of Vietnam, which requires the application of large American resources in the face of a concern to coin conventional warfare (but was also considered by the organized use of guerrilla techniques on US troops in a demonstration of the enemy's creativity in relation to opposing military superiority), since the use of nuclear weapons would receive retaliatory treatment from the USSR, interested in expanding its geopolitical control in South Asia. Another example is that

---

[44] *Ibidem*

of the Soviet missiles in Cuba which, if installed, would have fundamentally altered the balance of power in Latin America. Conventionally, the Cuban war would not present problems for more industrialized countries such as Mexico, Venezuela, or Brazil. Castelo Branco addresses the relationship between security and development as an increase in the country's economic capacity. This brings us to the consideration of the interrelationship between security and economic development.

Making the relation between economic capacity and military effectiveness that has varied over time, with the exception of naval warfare that would have required a certain degree of technological development, he explains that primitive wars relied more on individual aggressiveness, the genius of commanders, and the availability of human masses than with logistical capacity and the economic base.

The industrial revolution would have made the war much more technical, which would accentuate the importance of economic development as an element of security. In this way, this would be a result of the capacity for industrial mobilization and support logistics. Such a technique would be reaching its apogee in the nuclear age. Paradoxically, however, special conditions created by the "balance of terror" of the atomic age, to which Churchill referred, would, for two reasons, allow for a "temporary divergence between degree of development and war potential."

Firstly, since a direct nuclear confrontation became almost impossible, the antagonisms between the great powers would be channeled into peripheral wars of the type of war of liberation or revolutionary war, in any case, of localized war. "These are based less on economic mobilization than on the ideological stiffening of the population; reduce the logistical effort by parasitic infiltration in the community itself."

Secondly, because in the case of the use of nuclear weapons, if the surprise were preserved, there would be no time for industrial and economic mobilization. "Conceivably, a small country, possessing a small atomic arsenal and nuclear cargo shipment capability, could, in a short time, destroy the industrial superiority of a more resourceful antagonist."

Of course, this hypothesis, which is not very plausible, does not negate the advantages of industrial superiority, because the stronger country would probably also have better detection and greater aggressive arsenal, reducing the surprise factor and allowing the timely exercise of the capacity to retaliate.

This approach of Castelo Branco alludes to a military superiority associated with an industrial superiority. The Cold War superpower duel also well discriminated who possessed such superiority, evidently valued by the capabilities of the leading bloc countries. In this logic, the attachment to one's external policies would serve as a complement to the structural deficiencies of their satellite countries in the perspective of total war.

Non-alignment could entail easy retaliation denounced as the case of Cuba's missiles, allowing a country of less expressive industrial park than the opponent would enjoy the technological advantages of association with one of such block leaders. On the other hand, industrial development was already the preaching of the military elite since the first Vargas government.

The establishment of arms policy was a goal coveted by the military segment as a way of projecting it in the context of Brazilian society. In his vision of security and international politics, Castelo Branco[45] goes on to explain that "in an economically and socially interdependent world national security cannot be achieved on an exclusively internal basis. In addition, the means to save defense spending through schemes and also financing, funds to capitalize and provide technology for economic development, should be sought abroad. The historical and geographical realities would have inscribed us in the security device of the hemisphere".

Such a device would provide an effective nuclear shield against whims of extracontinental aggression, unlikely in the face of the "balance of terror." Brazil would not have the economic and even the technical resources to create its own "nuclear deterrence," and if this were done, it would be done by sacrificing its economic development and standard of living.

He explains that "the continental security device, as well as the entire western world, is consensual and not taxing." Within it, there would be room for the exercise of true independence, whether for the assertion of a regional political hegemony, as is the case today in Western Europe, or for the free search for forms of political and economic organization and international contacts, with the sole exception of the regime communist, considered by the Declaration of Punta del Este, as "incompatible" with the inter-American system.

The truth is that neither superpower would accept impassively, whatever the Brazilian emotions and desires: a fundamental change in the balance of power in an area of vital interest. It is not for another reason that, after the Cuban episode, the conflicts would be located in peripheral areas.

Recognizing this fact of the problem, the interest of the American republics would be to prevent any unilateral intervention, not only because it would seriously undermine the principle of "collective action and responsibility", but because errors in the judgment and evaluation of social and political transformations could tragically confuse, "reformist non-communist left-wing governments, interested in social reform, without submission to extra-continental ideologies and without subversive aggression, with communist dictatorships." The lecturer comments on the existence of a world governed by the "balance of terror" and the inability not to connect with it. It justifies the affirmation for the need of Brazilian emancipation for the respect of the international community.

At this point, it is observed that the military proposal exceeds the borders, in the evolution and the prestige intended for the military institution by the projection of the country abroad. The very evocation for the interests of the inter-American community to converge on the agreement of hemispheric alignment, is already the expansion of the proposal for the other countries of the continent, acting as a great ally of the United States.

The exaggerated connotation used in the typical phraseology of the anti-Soviet discourse demonstrates the predilection by the USA, in that option, even underscoring the Brazilian historical-geographic affinity with that country. Castelo Branco continues[46] to set out more reasons for development to be encouraged within the context of hemispheric security: "The acceptance of the continental security system does not inhibit our independence to trade freely, to discipline the capitals we wish to receive to

---

45 *Ibidem*
[46] *ibidem*

aid our development, to import technology and equipment from the sources we prefer".

He says that his government was the one that extended the trade and the exchanges with the socialist area. Under the impact of nationalism and the tensions created by the process of industrialization and development, a polycentric tendency emerged in the Soviet bloc, whose first manifestations would be the Yugoslav and Hungarian cases, projected explosively by the Sino-Soviet conflict. East and West tended to restrict trade relations to the respective blocs as an obvious condition of avoiding narrowing that could lead to the rupture of the channel of ideological dependence.

We even observe the case of Cuba's economic blockade, after its adherence to the socialist system. Castelo Branco, however, tells us that trade relations will not be affected in the future, highlighting its government initiative to ensure trade with the socialist bloc.

Indeed, as a precedent for this approach, serious discussions about the need for foreign capital injections into Brazilian industrialization were fought between the nationalist military and anti-nationalist currents, developed in an important discussion forum of the Armed Forces in the 1950s - the Military Club[47].

Castelo Branco then considers the relationship between security and nationalism, explaining that insofar as it is used as an element of mobilization of the national effort, with the acceptance of the sacrifices that development demands, leading to the attenuation of class conflict, the nationalism is highly positive.

But vicious nationalism becomes highly negative not only from the point of view of economic development but also national security, as it is manipulated by certain groups to avoid competition and maintain a market position; in which it is used to hinder the importation of foreign technology and that keeps imprisoned mineral resources in the Brazilian soil until there is capital to explore; in which it is manipulated by the "alienated left" to prevent the strengthening of the capitalist economic system and democratic institutions of the West.

In the 1950s, there was a serious rivalry between the military. Some military believed that industrialization should come under the interventionist form of the Brazilian State and not through the transfer of American capital and technological resources.

For those opposed to the US transaction there was clear control of US foreign policy over Brazilian foreign policy that would result in less profitable positions for Brazil as it lacked the technology and resources to exploit its abundant mineral estates. The US had such advantages and in the Brazil-US Commission[48] the terms of

---

[47] Cf. Andrade Júnior, H. Matrizes ideológicas presentes no segmento militar brasileiro: O Caso do Clube Militar. Comunicação Livre. In: *Encontro Regional De História, 21-25 Agosto,* 2000, Universidade Federal Fluminense. Campus do Gragoatá, Niterói: UFF.

[48] The Commission was set up under the government of Eurico Gaspar Dutra when they had examined the possibilities for a closer relationship with the United States. Its creation coincides with the creation of the ESG (made up of anti-Vargas) and aimed to study the Brazilian situation, outlining a program of economic development. Bringing modern concepts of indicative planning and capitalist rationality to Brazil, its recommendations and projects were published in 17 volumes of 1953-54. Among the civil participants was eminent Brazilian economist Roberto Campos. To further deepen the relationship, see

exploration and use of the benefits were established. Castelo Branco was representative of the interests in favor of the trust and the American transference.

This wing in favor of economic alignment was also known as anti-nationalist. Looking for support for the project that would imply the close link between security and development maintained by centralized control system, Castelo Branco talks[49] about the relationship between federalism and security, considering that separatism are detrimental to national security policy.

In his view, the Brazilian federative system would have differed greatly from the historical conditions that could be seen in the construction of the U.S., whose political structure influenced the Constitution of 1891. In the Brazilian case, an essentially unitary system was reorganized into federative units, instead of what happened in the USA, where the federation was formed by the free and periodic emergence of new states. "From the point of view of national security, we must guard against centrifugal forces, translated into separatist movements that, fortunately with an inexpressive repercussion, have arisen throughout our history."

He points out as a precautionary measure against the spread of national unity a promotion of the reduction of economic imbalances between states and regions to avoid the economic and demographic scarcity of border areas through programs of colonization, deployment of transport and promotion of economic growth. His argument in favor of a centralist approach follows by a discourse that the demands of the modern world, the integration of its markets, need for the unified role of the federation for economic development, the emergence of techniques of global economic planning and instrumentation harmonization of monetary policy create "an almost universal tendency to strengthen central power".

In his vision of democracy and the role of the ESG criticizes populist solutions that could lead to illusions by the promise of the facilities of the free and "miraculous" democratic regime, restricting his fantastic projection for the discipline imposed to all freedom. It calls on ESG to fulfill its mission of combining "civilian and military talent for the application of a permanent and coherent doctrine of national security: that of combating pseudo nationalism and pseudo development."

Another view of the posture of the War College in relation to the doctrine of security and development can be observed in the interview with Idálio Sardenberg[50]. It says: "Created ESG, we dedicate ourselves to establish a doctrine of national security. At the time, the emphasis was on external security. Internal security was of very small importance. And we thought that external security would only be possible with the promotion of the country's development.

Without development there would be no security. In addition, he sees it as accidental, "the fact that the people who conspired, prepared the Revolution of 1964 were eventually linked to the ESG. "Commenting accidentally" an architecture as well

---

STEPAN, Alfred, *Op.cit.*, Ch. 8.

[49] *Op. cit.*

[50] The State of São Paulo, on April 27, 1980, under the title "ESG nasceu para favorecer desenvolvimento". Idalius Sardenberg was one of the designated officers to study ESG's design project, which involved establishing a connection with the US and learning the molds of the American National War College and implanting its fundamentals suited to Brazilian interests in the new school.

assembled as a force machine, is not without reason.

The analysis of the facts leaves no doubt of the internal divisions between the military segment and this is the counter-argument. The depth of discussions behind the scenes of the Military Institution, such as the case of the Military Club that explored ahead in this work, also helps to reflect on this. Thus, the responses to the Slavic discourse failed to satisfy, in those days of the interview. Many errors and abuses were covered up from the perspective of the Cold War.

Sardenberg defends himself as one of the founders of the ESG and one of those responsible for the initial direction of this project, showing in this interview an astonishing fugacity and contrariety regarding the inquiries of the journalists, who sought to explore them.

As president of Petrobrás, a position of trust in the mechanism of industrialization, he reveals information that is not very clear about his role and about the Brazilian industrial program as a matter of strategy. However, the usefulness of his discourse lies in the exploration of his contradictions, some of which have already been explored in this work. In such a light, Sardenberg says that the doctrine of security must be separated from the regime of force of 1964: "The doctrine of security has not kept revolutionary governments, nor is it responsible for errors or correctness. They kept up with their own momentum." He comments on interesting episodes of the military actor's involvement in the antecedents of the School and its doctrine. The main passages are thus transcribed:

The State of São Paulo Newspaper (ESP) - As one of the organizers of the Superior School of War, could you tell us what your remote origins were? What kind of concern, or what goal, led to the creation of the School?

Sardenberg(S)- Actually, I was one of the first to launch the idea of creating ESG. In spite of its evolution from 1930 onwards, it was not possible until the end of the 1940s, when ESG was created, to consider itself an independent nation, since it was unable to manufacture any weapon necessary for its defense.

Consequently, the country needed to create means for it to be able to manufacture its weapons in the future. For this, the way was to promote the development of the country. Country with industrial capacity produces arms easily, when necessary. One way to help the country get to that point would be to create a pro-development mindset. And it was not enough for the Armed Forces to think so. There had to be such an intention among civilians.

I thought it would be interesting to form a mixed group of military men and civilians from different backgrounds to exchange ideas and create a mentality. My first idea to realize this was to set up a research institute and then evolve into a school run by the Armed Forces.

I must make it clear that I did not think this all by myself, but debating and talking to my friends. Through this exchange of ideas, a whole group that shared that way of seeing Brazil was formed within the General Staff of the Armed Forces.

ESP- Who was this group?

S- Besides me, there were, among others, Colonels Orlando and Ernesto Geisel, General Heitor Ferreira and Couto e Silva Golbery.

ESP- Those goals that he set forth were fulfilled by the School founded under the direction of Marshal Cordeiro de Farias?

S- I think so. Once the School was established, we set about establishing a doctrine of

national security. At the time, the emphasis was on external security. Internal security
was of very small importance. And we thought that external security would only be
possible with the promotion of development (...).

ESP- Has the security concern preceded the development concern?

S- Development is a means of promoting and securing safety. He is an instrument. To
be safe, we had to be able to defend ourselves. For this, we needed weapons: tanks,
cannons, ships, submarines, airplanes, etc. At that time we did not have the capacity to
do any of this; today we can manufacture almost everything.

ESP- Did this military project implicitly include a political project?

S- No, absolutely. It included, perhaps, an economic project for the country's
development, but not a political one.

ESP- Anyway what was intended was a project that would affect the whole country...

S- Yes, with time. The idea was to train people who, in public office-deputies,
ministers, etc.-were aware that it was necessary to promote measures that would
develop the country so that it would have security in the future. That was the idea.

ESP- What was sought was the formation of an elite?

S- Not from an elite, but from a group that worked around that idea. I see this group in
the same way as the one that was, for example, dedicated to the eradication of various
ailments. All these groups in different fields were working, I understand like the one
from ESG, for the good of the country.

ESP- Let us say, then, that it was a question of raising the awareness of people with
responsibilities in public life and in the private sector for the importance of that
problem.

S- Exact, because it would not be us military that we would promote the development
of the national industry. It was necessary for politicians and businessmen to work in
this direction. For our part, we would say to them: "We need to have national weapons
and we want them to help us in that direction. We think that by being free of arms
imports we will be a country with greater international authority and this idea would
benefit the country as a whole".

ESP- That original idea evolved over time and eventually became a national political-
economic-military project. How did you see the inclusion of the political element in this
project? Do you think he was inscribed in the very dynamics of the original idea of the
ESG or did the School exorbitate what was expected of it?

S- It is not that the ESG has exorbitant, is that it has adapted to the new times, to the
new situations. The idea of ESG was that of the development of the country and no
intention was made to make any revolution to achieve this. The position of the School
was not and could not be that of all the forces of the country. These forces evolved in
parallel in different ways. If they have malfunctioned, it is not the fault of ESG.

ESP- What we want to say is that, in order to make this military goal of weapons and
security feasible, an economic proposal for development was reached and, in order to
make it viable, it would inevitably have to come to a political proposal. That is what
happened?

S- No, because there was never in the School, other than the revolution of 64 here, the
intention to advocate ideas about political organization. The behavior of different
sectors of the country led to the conjuncture of 1964. And the seriousness of the events
then occurred provoked new positions of the ESG. It was not that it had prepared

itself or intended to come to this-at least from my point of view-but it was brought to it by the request of the facts themselves.

ESP- In other words, would it have been the very evolution of the country that demanded ESG to become what it is today?

S- This is exactly how I see it at this point, because the School I knew had no political purpose at all. With the evolution of the facts, there is no other institution capable of thinking about these political problems to which they refer - ISEB was a civil institution that tried to do this, but did not continue - the School was in the condition of only organization with capacity to play this role. Then, the Revolution began to request the School for this type of studies.

ESP- The general, or almost general, opinion is that the ideological core of the Revolution of 64 is located in ESG. It may be that this idea is not true, but it is undeniable that it is widespread. The truth is that the main characters and ideas of the 64-although not all-move out of there.

S- This is a fact that happened by chance. Many elements who participated in the Revolution were eventually serving in the School or were originally from it. The fact that the people who conspired, prepared, and carried out the Revolution were eventually linked to ESG is an accident.

ESP- But were not they fruits of the ESG?

S- What was the fruit of the School was the intellectual formation they had in it. This intellectual formation led them, perhaps, to clash with that situation before 1964, which they considered to be contrary to the interests of the country.

ESP- From that original group he cited as an inspirer of the ESG, a prominent army minister came out - General Orlando Geisel, a president-general Ernesto Geisel and General Golbery, who is considered as one of the main political articulators of three revolutionary governments. Not to mention Marshal Castelo Branco and several other officers who occupied prominent posts and who were linked to ESG.

S- It's a coincidence. General Ernesto Geisel, for example, would be president in a situation like the one in which he was elected, even if he did not belong to ESG. General Médici was president without being of the ESG. General Golbery has been a great scholar of Brazilian problems since he was a lieutenant. He became interested in the School, participated in its foundation and served in it for a long time. But he has an important political past that is not confused with the School. It's his past, as a person. I distinguish General Golbery as a man who belonged to ESG.

ESP- There remains evidence that it was the ESG that established the National Security doctrine.

S- No. The doctrine of national security was not properly established by ESG. This is not a Brazilian peculiarity. All countries have their doctrine of safety. In fact, it should be made clear that, with or without ESG's security doctrine, the revolutionary governments would remain the same, just as Getulio remained without it. I think the security doctrine did not keep the revolutionary governments, nor is it responsible for their correctness or mistakes. They kept up with their own dynamics. ESG men who exercised or perform political functions of government must naturally have come to the ideas they studied and learned during the time they attended. In your training you must tell a lot about the time they spent in school and what they studied there. This was incorporated into the experience of each one of them. I'm not saying that they did not use it, but I do not think they were characters who only transcribed or performed the ideas of the School. They held positions in accordance with the dynamics of government and that of power. But I repeat, in the exercise of political positions their action must of course have suffered the influence of the period they spent in ESG.

ESP- To what facts do you attribute the shift from the emphasis of external security to internal security?

S- There has been a transformation in the world situation, which has resulted in the attempt to bring into the countries the possibility of subversion and consequent change of political orientation. In other words, by acting from the outside, one tried to influence internal elements so that they themselves promoted changes in the political orientation of Brazil, for example - which, as I said, had a small importance, when the School-passed to have a greater prominence.

ESP- Is the doctrine of security, with this new emphasis on internal security, expressed in the National Security Law?

S- No, there is confusion between security law and security doctrine. One thing has nothing to do with the other. The law of security is the law of security for the state. The doctrine of security refers to the general and international security that all countries use.

ESP- Do it clearly distinguish the security law from the doctrine of security?

S- Completely. The only thing that exists in common between them is, by chance, the name. The law of security is the law of security for the state. The doctrine of security refers to the general and international security that all countries use.

ESP- Does it not seem to him that after 1964 national security was confused with state security because of exceptional circumstances of crisis?

S- Yes, several times, and this is normal, both Brazil and elsewhere. State security is included in national security in such a way that many people it may seem honestly that both are one and the same.

ESP- Did you participate in the struggles for the creation of Petrobrás?

S- No. I just watched from the outside, but it was good, I thought that was a good solution.

ESP- Since Petrobrás was created, its administration has been almost exclusively in the hands of the military. What do you attribute it to?

S- First of all, it must be said that it was also run by some civilians who held its presidency. Secondly, I think those who could answer that would be the presidents who appointed the military. What I do know is that there has never been any imposition or claim in the Army for any position at Petrobrás or at any state-owned company. I do not know why the presidents thought it best to turn over Petrobrás' direction to the military.

ESP- You yourself were one of the servicemen who held the presidency of Petrobrás, hence our question.

S- It is true. At the time of the Juscelino government, one day he told me: "Colonel, I sent for him, because I took some information about him and would like to appoint him president of Petrobrás. Accept the invitation?" I replied that it depended and he wanted to know what: "It depends on the conditions that you establish to deliver me the company." His answer was ready: "I give you carte blanche." I accepted, of course, and he added: "with a restriction, which is a request I want to make you: that you produce more oil." I explained to him that he would do everything to fulfill his request, but that he could not guarantee anything, because the production of oil did not depend on people. "I know, Colonel, that this is random, that it depends a little (he made a gesture with his hand) from up there." I think it important to record President Juscelino's efforts to increase oil production in Brazil.

ESP- Was it at the time of his administration that the American geologist Walter Link ended his work in Brazil and made the famous report stating that there is no oil here?

S- It is true. Link was a very controversial personality because he was a foreigner. He had worked for "Esso" (Exxon Corp.) and perhaps for other foreign oil companies. So there was a certain reserve regarding him in the country, which made his presence damage the environment in Petrobrás, as well as the relationship of the company with the public. For these reasons, when his contract was terminated, I resolved not to renew it, although I had never known of any position adopted by him that would indicate a lack of commitment on his part to help solve Petrobrás problems in the search for oil. In addition, Petrobrás had already formed a good group of geologists, so we could do without your help.

ESP- Almost 30 years after the creation of Petrobrás, we still do not find oil in significant quantities. Will we have to come to the sad conclusion that the ill-fated "Mister Link" was right?

S- It is hard to say. Your report may be scientific, but it can also be fraught with a bit of hurt because your final essay was made after he left us. We may suddenly find oil. There are incredible cases of unexpected discoveries in oil history.

ESP- Was Petrobrás' creation, in the highly emotional climate in which it occurred, no more a political than an administrative act?

S- I do not believe. State-owned enterprises exist in several countries, even in the USA, to solve certain problems. There is no doubt that oil is a major problem, as is also electricity, and in developing countries these problems have been solved at the initiative of the state. See, next to Petrobrás, there is Eletrobrás. I think Petrobrás has been a very useful working tool for the country.

ESP- In recent years Petrobrás has been much more concerned with the production of derivatives from oil purchased outside to supply the market and with the diversification of its activities-distribution, petrochemicals, etc.-than with the prospecting of Brazilian territory, which is the purpose for which it was created. What do you think of that?

S- The argument that Petrobras should devote itself solely to finding oil has been repeated a lot. Now, in my view, it cannot withstand the least examination. If Petrobrás was exclusively engaged in prospecting - and since the discovery of oil is random - in two or three years it would have ended up with all the money it had and would have no means of recovering. Who thinks that Petrobrás should only do prospecting or it will the end? This is the fastest, most simple and most beautiful way to end it. At the same time as it seeks oil, it must produce the necessary resources for this task. If it does not produce these resources, it will not be the government that will dispose of them to deliver to it, as it has many other equally urgent and important tasks to take care of. How to produce these resources? Working side-by-side in those petroleum-related industrial activities that unlike their prospecting have no random character such as refining and petrochemical or commercial ones as products distribution. This is what produces the necessary resources for oil exploration. This has been the orientation of Petrobrás and I do not think it has diminished the effort that should be devoted to the prospecting. During my management, for example, I doubled oil production. What can not be forgotten is that, as I told President Juscelino, it is well known that the discovery of oil is random; it does not depend only on our effort. In Argentina, for example, oil was found by chance. The first well they discovered was by luck. They were digging for water.

ESP- But it is true that, in recent years, Petrobrás invests less in prospecting than in other related tasks.

S- I do not think it neglected her prospect. What happens is that a company can make a bigger effort in one sector than in the other. This emphasis on one or another sector may vary depending on who directs it. But overall I think he did not neglect the prospecting. The truth is that the oil crisis began in 1973 and everyone was pointing Petrobrás as responsible for our difficulties in this sector, as if it could guess what would happen.

ESP- Are you in favor of risk contracts?

S- I see them as one more research tool. As the resources that Petrobrás has to invest in research are limited, despite the effort it makes, we must use other means to discover oil and among them are the risk contracts. I think they are acceptable as an instrument.

ESP- What is the judgment of the Juscelino government today?

S- It was the government of Juscelino that inaugurated in the country the developmental orientation that advocated by the Superior School of War from 1949. I believe that it corresponded to the yearnings of the ESG in several aspects.

ESP - What was your participation, after the resignation of Jânio Quadros, in the acceptance by the military ministers of the formula of the parliamentary regime, that made possible the solution of the crisis, with the possession of João Goulart?

S- I did not have a direct participation in this episode, which was normal, because the problem was at a higher level. But as I was and am a friend of Marshal Denys, I had a personal conversation with him. I called his attention to the danger of fighting two chains-the one that was contrary and the one that was favorable to the possession of João Goulart-dividing the country into two opposing camps, which would be highly detrimental. Within this idea, I asked him to examine the possibility of resolving the crisis through an agreement between the parties.

ESP-What was your position during the Goulart administration?

S- During the Goulart administration I was serving in military units, away from politics, wishing that he would arrive to the end and presidential elections would be held, so that the guidelines could be taken back to President Juscelino's government.

ESP- Would you prefer then that there had not been a break of 1964?

S- Yes. I would prefer that there was no need for a movement that would disrupt democratic evolution.

ESP - Above all, since the Republic, the military has always exerted a great influence on Brazilian politics; influence that grew extraordinarily from 1964. How is this phenomenon explained?

S- Perhaps one of the explanations is that the Armed Forces is a corporation based on hierarchy and discipline and operating in the direction set by its chiefs. Except for the church, which is an organization that works more or less in the same way, we do not have institutions organized in the country, besides these two. Party organizations, for example, have many disagreements, which makes it difficult for them to solve any problem given the variety of opinions that surround them. Already in the Armed Forces no. Once they are convinced of a certain thesis, they act and comply rigidly with the determinations that come from their superiors. This naturally gives them a certain predominance over other currents.

ESP- To a great extent, is this great political influence of the Armed Forces due to the weakness of the Brazilian parties?

S- Yes, to a large extent it seems to me that this is it.

ESP- Do you give the Armed Forces a missionary vocation?

S- I would say that the military consider its mission the defense of the country and the Brazilian society. This is part of the military profession.

ESP- What image do the military make of this country and society, whose defense consider their mission?

S- This image is, as I said at the beginning, the happiness of the Brazilian people. The military considers itself Brazilian people. He is an element that speaks on behalf of his people, defends them, suffers with them, fights for them. This is the mentality of the Brazilian officer and when he wants the development of the country is for the benefit of the people and not of him in the Armed Forces. The military thinks it must have an obligation to help the people in every way and does everything possible to do so. If you convince the military that a certain thing is certain, good for the people and that the people need it, it will naturally adopt it with a critical spirit.

ESP-Does he think himself the guardian of all this? That is, the Brazilian military is not exclusively concerned with the territorial defense of the country.

S- This is a part.

ESP- And the other?

S- The other is the defense of Brazilian laws, institutions and traditions. It is not that he thinks himself the guardian. He feels obliged to help in the defense of all this. He does not consider himself the owner of the ball, he is one of the team players.

ESP- In this perspective, does not it act even against the will in political longings?

S- The military has a more general view than a political party. Perhaps it was closer to the truth to say that they would be a kind of party confederation.

ESP-Many people are concerned about the fall of the social cadets of the Army cadets. How do you see this problem?

S- I have not the slightest concern in that regard. I was director general of Army education and worked to expand administration in military schools of elements of all classes and all states. On the other hand, my idea was to ensure the admission of elements from the most different sectors of the population: farmers, workers, professionals, civil servants, etc., so that the Army could become the most representative of nationality.

ESP-This is an ideal picture. Our question is whether reality does not contradict it today.

S- Yes, this is the ideal we must work for. I have been away from this problem for some years now and I do not know whether the reality

ESP- Do you accept the long-held thesis that has been strongly insisted that the Armed Forces would assume the role of moderating power of the emperor in the Republic?

S- It's true. They have exercised this Power. I think this is a historical fact that one cannot fail to recognize. But the Armed Forces use this power in terms, because they do not appoint senators or prime ministers, as the Emperor did. They have naturally been led to exercise a kind of moderating power that seeks to balance the different social tendencies of the country. Perhaps because of those features that I mentioned earlier and that distinguish the Armed Forces, that is, hierarchy, discipline and unity of action.

ESP- In the interventions prior to 1964, the military retired immediately after the reorganization of the situation within of conditions that they considered convenient, and leaving the country under a regime of constitutional normality. That was what characterized the Moderating Power. But in 1964 they are installed directly in power. Does not it seem to him that in this case the limits of the Moderating Power have been exceeded?

S- Yes, it seems that he was a little stronger than the moderating power.

ESP- Was he not so moderate?

S- Yes, he was not as moderate as he was if you wish. But the circumstances were also not moderate. It seems to me that circumstances forced this.

ESP- How did you see the opening process initiated by former President Geisel, which presupposed a "return to the barracks", to use a very used expression then?

S- I think that expression misrepresents the facts. It should be avoided because it gives the impression that the military is out of the barracks when they are not. It gives an erroneous idea of the Brazilian reality. The military is all in the barracks. Some, almost all reserve officers are holding civilian positions.

ESP- When it comes to "returning to the barracks," it means moving away from the military in the political process.

S- I think it is appropriate for the military government and parliament, also as there always was. I find it interesting and advantageous for the country. I really think it was not a good thing to establish that the elected military would go into the reserve. They should only be licensed to be deputies or senators, because it is important that this exchange, this exchange of ideas between civil and military, for the development of the country.

ESP- Do you think there may be some setback in the process of opening?

S- this is probable, although there are always risks, as in everything in life, because one does not live in absolute security. The government's work is all about building a strong party to support it, which it hopes to achieve in the 1982 elections. The timing is difficult, especially because of the problems caused by inflation, but it is working to win electoral victory.

ESP- Does this short stay in the various stages of the career in the general one, have as a consequence the non-formation of leaderships in the Armed Forces?

S- Exactly, leadership is lost in this system, and they can be very beneficial. There is a time when good leadership in the Armed Forces can lead to good results. Leadership is no longer formed today, because officers have no time to become known, not because their merits and their preparation are less than those of previous generations. In my time there were officials known nationally.

ESP- If the armed forces exercise a kind of moderating power, they also have a political function, in addition to the purely professional one. Does this lack of leadership in your cadres do not weaken your ability to perform the political function?

S- It weakens. That system is a sure way to end the Moderation Power of the Armed Forces.

ESP- Would you rather I did not end?

S- What I think is that the Armed Forces still have a part to play in the development of

Brazil. It cannot be forgotten that they have helped a lot in this direction and can continue to do so for a long time.

ESP- Is it favorable to the creation of the Ministry of Defense?

S- I am in favor of the Armed Forces General Staff as it now exists, as its chief having minister status. Each of the three forces has its own characteristics and it is very difficult to administer them all through a single Ministry. The need for coordination that should exist between them, without interference in the administrative and organizational part of each one, is satisfied by the EMFA, which seems to me an excellent solution.

ESP- Resistance to the Ministry of Defense was not due, in part, to fear

S- No, because the Minister of the Army can be a civilian, the Navy and the Air Force, too.

The ideological matrices in relation to the doctrine of National Security

Guita Debert (1986, p. 102) says that, in general, "there is an absence of consensus in the characterization of the various political-ideological tendencies that are supposed to be present in the history of the Brazilian Armed Forces." It goes on to analyze Vanda Aderaldo[51] which points to two tendencies identified by the opposition between nationalism and anti-nationalism or democratic and anti-democratic.

Edmundo Campos (1976), on the other hand, as already shown, considers DSN as an expression of the generation that fights for the modernization of the armed forces, assuming the set of demands that, since the 1930s, had been placed by the group formed around Góes Monteiro. Another author, Alexandre de Barros[52], considers that it would be possible to think of ESG as the "locus of symbiosis between this group pointed out by Edmundo Campos and the generation of lieutenants of 1922 who had been systematically deprived of power every time he was near him" (1979, p. 102). Completing the circle, three tendencies were identified by Clóvis Brigagão[53], among which we can observe the framework of the Brazilian National War College.

- Nationalists, whose history dates back to the uprisings of 20, under the impulse of the liutenentist' movement. They participated actively in the Revolution of 1930, forming a group that proposed a greater participation of the urban layers and a new policy for the working one. In the 1950s they emerged as a more cohesive group, having as a flag of struggle an economic nationalism. Its central forum was the Military Club where they were armed for the creation of Petrobrás. In the period of 1961-64, they supported all programs aimed at increasing the participation of the State in foreign investments. With regard to their conceptions of international relations, they had great distrust of the American presence in Latin America. They believed that the high profits obtained in Brazil were spent in the United States in the Defense system. They criticized the type of division of the world proposed by the cold war and

---

[51] *Op.cit.*

[52] BARROS, Alexandre. (1979). *Formando Elites.* Jornal da Tarde, 25 Ago 79

[53] BRIGAGÃO, Clovis. (1978). *Brazil's Foreign Policy: The Last 15 years* .Mimeo, Institute of Latin American Studies, Stockholm.

claimed an independent economic policy, considering that the USA was the greatest threat to world peace, thus putting itself against an automatic alignment with American politics;

- Internationalists, known as the Sorbonne elite and defined as the best organized group, with connections at the highest levels both nationally and internationally. They had common characteristics that identified them. They commanded the FEB, attended the same schools in France and the United States, formed the ESG, planned the João Goulart movement and took office after the Revolution of 1964, supported the creation of the Inter-American Peace Force and the invasion of Dominican Republic and, in retirement, had high positions in multinational and state-owned Brazilian companies. Their ideology was largely anti-communist, and although they claimed confidence in democracy, they had total distrust of any kind of popular participation;

- Hard Core, mixing authoritarianism, nationalism, Bismarckian innovations, corporatism and populism. It was made up of middle-ranking officers, mostly colonels and captains. For the most part, they participated in the democratic crusade in the 1950s. They tried several times to overthrow civilian governments and managed to function as the Operational Armed Forces that did the coup. They had the common characteristics of not being of the FEB (Brazilian Expeditionary Force in II WW), were not the most graduated, did not belong to the elite of the ESG, some were trained in the US War College, but most attended the US Military School of The Americas, located in the zone of the Panama Canal, school that specialized military in the combat to the insurrection. From the ideological point of view, they wanted the modernization of the country from top to bottom, with charismatic ingredients, in order to gain popular support. They distrusted the "politicians", considering them corrupt and inefficient in the direction of the State. They conceived the international system as a group of autonomous nations struggling against each other for political and military economic advantages. They were fighting for nationalist and patriotic measures that included direct actions against foreign interests, even in the case of the United States (Brigagão, 1978).

3 THE ESG DOCTRINE AND THE AGRARIAN QUESTION

A brief sketch of the state of the art on the Brazilian agrarian question

The survey of the main works and their considerations in the Brazilian agrarian context is fundamental to adjust the development of the ideas coming from ESG to the agrarian question. In general, as has been intensively explored, the Cold War environment is one of the main documentary sources used in this work.

To elaborate in this format, although historical returns are necessary for the explanation of the mechanisms of agrarian political action that precede the scope of the research, it pretends to show a power game that is profoundly influenced by the archaisms of an agrarian structure addicted and still sick until the present day. As has already been written, there was no military current in favor of Brazil's pro-agricultural demonstration, and this seems to be important for mapping how military approaches on the agrarian problem go.

Thus, under the agrarian sociology, as for the members of the "Itatiaia" Group[54] (Nelson Werneck, Hélio Jaguaribe, Roland Corbisier and others), precursor of the Higher Institute of Brazilian Studies (ISEB), the importance of his works as opposing theorists to what Castelo Branco, Golbery do Couto or Costa e Silva preached. ISEB was created in 1955, attached to the Ministry of Education and Culture, in the government of João Café Filho to be "a permanent center for post-university level political and social studies with the purpose of encouraging the study, teaching and dissemination of social sciences, especially of sociology, history of economics and politics, especially for the purpose of applying the categories and data of these sciences to the analysis and critical understanding of the Brazilian reality aiming at the elaboration of theoretical instruments that allow the encouragement and promotion of development national", according to Article 1 of its statute. It followed the line of the IBESP, Brazilian Institute of Economy, Sociology and Politics, and its national-developmental ideology was predominant for its extinction in 1964, with the regime of force from 1964.

---

[54] A group of intellectuals based in Rio de Janeiro in the early 1950s (and meeting in Itatiaia-RJ) sought to convince the then Education Minister, Cândido Mota Filho, of the need for the government to constitute a place of study for the demands of the capitalist modernity.

The role of Roland Corbisier in his "Reformation or Revolution" assumes the call of attention to the addictive and binding condition of the reforms proposed for the period (1968, p. 6), considered by him, "incapable of blending agrarian structure", also deleterious. In the mid-1960s he suggested revising the Land Statute "to make him able to liquidate the monopoly of land" (1968, p. 115), enabling the creation of new settlements assisted by modern technology and placing them subordinate to national capitalism, "since they allow to increase the consumer population and collect more for the industry, in the form of diversified agricultural inputs". In fact, in its approach, it does not only focus on such advantages as demands on Brazilian capitalism, interested in the domestic market, nor does it exhaust them with the diversification of cultures for the supply of large urban centers, but because it is not tolerable, that millions of Brazilians, continue to live as pariahs, misery, ignorance, disease, hunger, deprived of everything we consider indispensable to our own lives (1968, p.115).

Celso Furtado, on the same national-developmental strand, writing "A Project for Brazil" shows that there existed in the country's economic system a structural deformation that translated into the profile of global demand (1968, p. 15). Such deformation, he said, was responsible for the slow penetration of technological progress in our economy and for the scarce diffusion of the fruits of productivity increases. In making such a synthesis, he considered the positive performance of the economy of the previous two decades and, at that moment, saw a decline in the yield of the policy of import substitution. In fact, due to certain structural peculiarities, the Brazilian economy was not in a position to benefit in the way that it was worth, when considering the natural resources, "the size of its population and the level of development achieved at that point. It proposed, among other correctives, a modification of the demand profile, which allows raise the rates of saving and investment" (1968, p. 14).

The problem, which is articulated with the structural deformation, includes the agrarian structure reflected on the profile of this demand, revealing a significant sum of the effect of the mismatch on the socio-economic field, with the immeasurable waste of labor and the low efficiency in the use of capital by the organization of Brazilian agriculture. He suggested that such a problem should be tackled by an effort to raise the standard of living of the lower third of the rural population in the short term, whose "extreme poverty and food shortages are in themselves serious obstacles to raising productivity in the agricultural sector" (p.15).

In addition, it focused on a decisive prognosis: "without a direct attack on the large farms, the deep deformation that exists in this face of the economic system will not be eliminated" (p.16). As a final synthesis of its argument, it characterized our economy as dependent, that is, an economy where technological progress is created by development, or rather by structural changes that initially appear alongside demand, "while in developed economies technological progress is, in itself the source of development" (p. 23), a condition that is responsible for the proposal that the author argued and needed to provide a new rhythm for national development.

João Carlos Monteiro de Carvalho in his work, "The Peasants in Brazil", in this discussion, explains that peasants, a basic component of the peasantry, since its inception have been a marginalized element of the global productive process, "having no importance as be productive for the economy the one of the Country" (1978, p.118). In fact, João Carlos explains that "the main characteristic of the Brazilian peasantry is that of economic, social and political subordination in relation to other categories" (1978, p. 117), with a predominantly pre-capitalist level of interaction. Such an analysis would justify effective mechanisms for the effectively capitalist alignment of the peasantry and woefully left it in even smaller proportions.

Another work, Moisés Vinhas, "The Earth, Man and the Reforms," again expresses the inconsistency of the reformist argument for use abusive of rhetoric and panacea to the problem of the field, well positioned in the period under examination. Proposing the conditions for an authentic agrarian reform, the author comments on the need for it to take place on a democratic basis (although the concept must be considered in its ideological context of the regime of force), "avoiding the manipulation of the State (1980, p.140), illegitimate form of driving", since it would discriminate the categories directly involved in the reform proposal. The rationale for some of its reasons lies in the agro-capitalist order that leads to dependence on foreign capital and national financial resources for the import of food products. In any case, this arrangement leads "to a significant fall in the participation of the primary sector in the national production as a whole, leading to scarcity in several branches of agricultural production in the line of export and domestic supply" (1980, p. 02), harming industrial businesses.

The study of agrarian sociology for José Murilo de Carvalho, recorded in the book "The Construction of the Order", the bureaucracy's view would be that in countries of late bourgeois revolution (especially those of colonial origin and the remnants of the socialist revolution), the impact of political elites on the formation of the state tends to be potentially greater due to the absence of a cohesive and national ruling class. In the Brazilian case, for the author, "the homogeneity of the elite (1996, p. 34) was one of the factors that contributed to provide the political system with characteristics distinct from those found in countries from the Spanish colonizing influence". Among the characteristics that can be seen, the author highlights the "small incidence of intra-internal conflicts, political unity and the maintenance of a stabilized civil order" (1996, p. 103).

As a consequence of its homogenization, the elite would also have contributed to solidifying the structure of domination of the slave order and opened the door to the pattern of authoritarian reformism. Is it possible to identify the author's concern to correlate the elite, socialized by education with the other sectors of the ruling class (seeking a symbiotic relationship?), considering the central problems of slavery and land. The author's understanding of this interconnection lies in the co-opting of potential enemies of the system, which eludes access to power, but is more effective against the inflexibility of the thesis of a bureaucratic state, as it increases the time of permanence of the situation's elite.

The argument he maintains is that the adoption of a monarchical solution in Brazil, the maintenance of the ex-colony's unity and the construction of a stable civilian government were a good part of the type of political elite that existed at the time of independence, Portuguese colonial policy.

Ideological homogeneity and training will reduce conflicts between the elite and provide the conception and capacity to implement a particular model of political domination (Carvalho, 1996). In the very context, the author says that the political elite, with an emphasis on the magistrates, had to compromise with the owners, to obtain an arrangement of seeming order, though profoundly unjust. As an example, "the National Guard showed such bargaining power when it inserted in its body personalities of the rural aristocracy interests"(1996, p.142).

The social cohesion of the elite tended to isolate it, however, from new sectors that came to light with the socio-economic transformations of the Second Reign (Dom Pedro II).

As a consequence, there was centralization of power in the political and legal sphere, generating manifest discontent in popular movements. The accumulation of civil servants and administrative activities at the central government level, "their reduced presence at the provincial level and almost absence at the local level, partially describes the scenario and characterizes that the concentration of power was a fact (1996, p.137), with degrees of centralization different tasks".

The author noted a weakness of elite reproduction in producing other elites adapted to new tasks, becoming a victim of their own success. In the logic of the empire, magistrates were related to farmers and in the republic the military polarized with the farmers, evidencing a conservative modernization.

The Brazilian bureaucracy, on the other made, evidences to the author the weakness of the Portuguese, considering the absence of the agrarian aristocracy interposed to the interests of the royalty, in the Portuguese case. Based on the thesis that the greater the success of the bourgeois revolution, the lower the weight of functionalism, confirms the lack of feudalism in our case and creates spaces for the doctrine of homogenization in order to better and greater process of state formation. Carvalho (1996, p. 36) comments on a "transfer of possibilities from the agrarian-slave system to the elite peripherals: professional civil servants who used it as an instrument of social ascension".

The confusion that the author points out from the Brazilian bureaucracy to the political elite, which generates contradictory interpretations about the nature of the elite, the bureaucracy and the state itself (1996, p. 37), "mobilizes the thesis that supports the existence of a bureaucratic statist structure preconceived, but rather a political conception of hierarchical power".

He points out that the imperial bureaucracy "was not stately, but it had its own rationality" (1996, p. 149)and emphasizes that the context of the empire was favorable to the conversion of bureaucracy into political elite. Parliament exceeds politics as an aristocratic activity exercising control over bureaucracy. It does not understand the bureaucracy as autonomous (see elite socialization process).

In any case, it has already been explained that the process favored the social mobility of the elite peripherals, generating ambiguity based on the actions of these public employees, excluded from the agrarian-export mechanism.

The fact is that Carvalho is "against the thesis of the bureaucratic state", defended so vehemently by Faoro (below). It qualifies him as liberal democrat (1996, p. 38), although he is clearly Iberian.

Carvalho demonstrates that the homogenized elite behave like an element of modernization and its base is Portuguese that advances in a continuum of the relations of the Portuguese elite with the Brazilian elite and its patrimonial ties. Carvalho's modernizing and pragmatic proposal is the only one that qualifies the dynamism proposed by his thesis. Curiously, it does not recognize the warlordism present in Latin America in Brazil, by the specificity of our patrimonial relations, although the south of the country is filled with warlordism evidences.

For Raymond Faoro, in The Owners of Power, the pressure from top to bottom is the main thrust of his argument. Based on a state model of Thomas Hobbes and supported by Weber's thesis of the need for an effective bureaucratic basis for the functioning of the state machine, even if distanced from the capitalist spirit and ethics, it creates spaces for an argument based on centralism with roots in the Peninsula Iberian Such centralism, which is a legacy for the author, is reflected in Brazil with the existence of political estates - categories that are closely dependent on the central and intensely co adjuvant power - that, by their bureaucratic nature, arbitrate the nation and social classes, being regulators of the economy and owners of national sovereignty.

It is a form of stratification with more closed layers than social classes and more open than castes, that is, it has greater social mobility than in the caste system, and less social mobility than in the social class system. It is a type of stratification still present in some societies. In these societies, from the present or the past, the individual from birth is obliged to follow a predetermined lifestyle, recognized by law and generally linked to the concept of honor, although there is some social mobility.

The state, thus bureaucratically organized by estates, would confirm the precocity of the Portuguese conception, for in the process of domination of the Portuguese crown there is the mark of submission of the nobility to the King's request to centralize power, leaving the elite without its own light.

The reality of this environment conducive to the submission of an absolute power in the domain of the national will, characterizing a constant duality between the tax and the liberal, becomes the stage of its discussion. For the author, by extending his frontiers with navigations, lacking the exercise of his advanced conception of the State, Portugal founds a pre-capitalist frontier as politically oriented capitalism and distinctly distinct from the Anglo-Saxon, by the mercantile and non-industrial option that it adopted. The burden of privileges and concessions that moves the machine from the dependence of the political elite to the dictates of the "prince", for Faoro, is vivified in the plane of action by patrimonialism - basic political organization that closes itself with the bureaucratic state – "which gives the sense of the appropriation of the position and not of the rational apparatus" (1997, p. 84).

The authoritarianism present in this sense orders the independent development of the logic of the market and, even in the moments that the economic presupposition is very evident, stands for a conservative network of dependence on the benefits of the State. That form of patrimonial domain clarifies "when the Chief of Staff appears with the king, extending through the territory and influencing political units" (1997, p.736). If the administrative structure was lacking, the dispersed leadership assumed a patriarchal attitude, clearly observable at the farmer's or colonel's command.

On the process of patrimonial dominion, Faoro points out, through the estate economic opportunities are appropriated that are distributed discretionally in a confusion between the public and the private, maintaining, nevertheless, its original operational characteristics, because, in the end, personal patrimonialism converges to state patrimonialism. For Faoro, the mechanism persists to the point of not changing the foundations of society, contrary to the liberal argument, since it considers it artificial to the Brazilian case, not only because of the lack of feudalism that justifies it, but because of our agricultural and non-industrial vocation.

The São Paulo case, which gives rise to this argument, assumes the cause of the federalist interest, despised by the author, since, despite bringing changes in production in the classical ways, it was unable to transform institutions.

Simon Schwartzmann, in "The Bases of Brazilian Authoritarianism", however, considers the change brought about by the role of São Paulo in the traditional Brazilian centralism.

Based on the regionalist, federalist approach, it verifies a new tendency of reorganization of the national politics: "neopatrimonialism, proposing that its overcoming to the patrimonialism can be an alternative to cross its heavy, imbibed and inefficient structure of bureaucratic juice, nourished by a system of values outmoded and conservative" (1988, p.10), "leading to a transition, intermediate position between centralism and economic liberalism". In this way, he believes that São Paulo represents an advance that brings changes to the structure of state and society in relation to its classic position of planning and interventory function in economic and social life, valuing local patrimonialism and Americanism.

It seems that Simon provokes a re-reading of the society using the vision of Faoro, because it considers it doctrinal point of departure for the argumentation. It seeks to read the macro-structural context post-1964, observing the new dynamics of the country that concentrates in the great capitalist centers of the power. He agrees with Faoro against the Marxist thesis, since "Brazilian elites cannot be understood from economic interests, and such, show certain autonomy of them" (1988, p. 33). The thesis of authoritarianism, however, for Simon, must be reviewed, since in the context of the work he believes he has fulfilled his function namely to carry out, in his own way, "the process of transition of the Brazilian economy from a protocapitalist system to a full capitalist economy" (1988, p. 20). In prophesying the end of authoritarianism, as a necessity for government, he says that, without a doubt, it is a powerful condition for the country, but it can be overcome, "having brought deleterious effects to society, symbiotically united to the state" (1988, p. 26).

Simon, to support the overcoming of capitalist ethics in the Brazilian environment, seeks the thesis of de-westernization of the process, reflected by the absence of national authenticity and identity. In this case, he appropriates Max Weber for patrimonial domination (1988, p. 60), establishing that the traditional gives way to the modern, in the presence or not of feudalism. However, he explains that the neo-patrimonialism he advocates is different from the "outside the West" model, because in our case, there is a strong survival of the traditional forms that mask it. This leaves doubts as to the Eastern nature that he advocates. In order to qualify the Brazilian domination, he criticizes the term "bureaucratic state" used by Faoro with the aforementioned discussion, Carvalho (1979) considers a social stratum without properties and that has no social honor for its own merit and uses the concept to base its analyzes on local power, showing the value of privatist actions of authority for the formation of the National State.

These actions, federalists, for Simon, escape the rule of coalition between the rural oligarchy and the state, because they led to the segmentation of interests, and, as a rule, were administered by the central power in a fragmented way (1988, p. 99). In seeking to emphasize this phenomenon from the bottom up, evidenced in his cited work (Chapters 3, 4 and 5), shows the necessity of the coexistence of the bureaucratic and patrimonial state with the private, individualistic and privatist sector, aiming at the construction of a new the relationship between State and Society, because, for the author, unlike Faoro, the particular interferes with the State's action.

Maria Silvia de Carvalho, in "Free Men in the Escravocrata Order" (1976), brings Agrarian Sociology to think about configu in order to examine the nature of the state and class structure, as they were described as manifest ambiguity in our history, and which can be perceived from the existence of two opposing principles: life and goods.

There is a visible theme of personal dependence ("the four-year rally"), being a study referenced in the Weberian field, as well as Faoro, differing in the approach, which is not that of the State, but that of the Society. It is possible to identify a strong neighborhood with the work of Oliveira Viana in "Southern Populations of Brazil", although the author does not mention it.

It is considered the possibility, however, of having failed to take it into account, since Raimundo Faoro, in 1960, was a peripherally known author, also unnamed by it. From the analysis of Maria Silvia's work, a very interesting analytical maneuver emerges as the author skirts the strong and dominant axis of the slave-slaves relationship to study an interstitial population of white, free, and poor men, who are not integrated into the merchant population, but classified into the production of means of subsistence, which is marginal to the agro-exporting effort of the slave-owning large farm, articulated to Western capitalism.

Curiously, slaves, properly speaking, are absent from Maria Silvia's work, corroborating to emphasize the defended bias, with a view to the originality of the approach. On slavery, she considers it as the support of the capitalist structure, but when he analyzes the large farm, he divides it into two segments of study, explaining that the principles of commodity production add to the slave's dependence on the master, but the principles of production of means of life allies you to a relationship with free, white and poor men.

Such men, observes Maria Silvia, through surveys of criminal cases, live in cooperation; in reciprocal complementation marked by poor culture in a scenario of interpersonal violence. Due to the marginality of the situation in which they live, when they are excluded from the agrarian-export system, they provide services without formal structure or codes of discipline, affecting the optimization of results. Marginalization, explains Maria Silvia (1976) leads this man to live by favor, by the grace of the Lord in a world of large farms, carefully articulated to mercantile interests. From this point of view, it is a marginal on the dominant side of the large farm; characters of the scarcity, reflecting a very particular behavior of defense to this isolation. Focusing from bottom to top, Silvia coincides with the meaning of Oliveira Viana, diverse from Faoro.

The limited space of these people does not create conditions for associations of interests or morals: it is people without social identity, without appearance, without social relation. She explains that, for example, the merchants or troopers can even ascend socially without participating in the status provided by an economic category: they float without tradition according to demand, showing provisional and informal cooperation, but disqualified as a class. Seeking to synthesize the thesis of the author, it is visible the approach that defends of a rational legal order within this world of mutual dependence, that is, society positions itself with rationalized delay in favor of the expansion of capitalism. Moreover, the personal power evidenced in a patrimonialism exercised from the bottom up by the logic of the market prevents the existence of the class society. Such a society is warmly influenced by the state, legally competent to organize it, but ineffective by its commitment to the capitalist system.

With Oliveira Viana, in the book "Southern Populations of Brazil" (1933) comes a sociological vision of the rural world that holds in the premise of opposition between a legal country and a real one, that is, an environment of power conflicts that denotes the victory of localism in the realm of private power.

Despite this emphasized angle of observation, it seems that the author develops a discourse of Iberian bases without doctrinal affectation to Americanism. It shows the distance between Brazilian institutions and those, constituted of individuals and people, by the bad adaptation of the Anglo-Saxons to Brazilian case. It even emphasizes that the Republic would have returned the political culture of the colonial world, through legalism and coronelism, evidencing the strong Iberian base.

In this context, "the large farm of the colonial period summarizes and absorbs life around, leaving no room for the small and medium-sized owner, who end up living independently in their small domain" (1933, p. 75), and also reflects their autarchic aspect that formation of a rural middle class.

Commenting on the fact that servile work becomes repulsive to the free man, he explains that the "free settler, who is a plebeian condition because he cannot be a worker or owner of the large farm" (1933, p. 84), opens spaces for social relations that do not induce soli social responsibility.

If solidarity is impaired, however, clan relations that evidence social not supportive open doors to warlordism. In short, it observes a tendency towards despotism as a limit situation, motivated by the localism already mentioned that leads to the nickname of barbarism and the consequent fact of social not supportive.

Besides the reported picture, the author highlights "the extreme mobility of these discontented human groups, as a consequence of the exclusionary social organization" (1933, p. 116). It reflects that such non-fixation of the residents is also motivated by their economic condition which compels them emigrating from the small farms in search of a better situation.

The loose relationship of dependence between the farmer and his farmer shows, according to the author, "a Brazilian singularity when compared to the European social structure" (1933, p. 174) and defines the relation of interdependence and solidarity as temporary, fragmented and unstable, characterized by the fact that "our rural worker can live perfectly without the farmer's employer's protection" (p.174), discarding the hypothesis of feudalism in our environment.

With such a lack of feudalism reinforcing his thesis of independence, he emphasizes, from observations on "the large farm and not on the State, that the self-regulation is harmful (against liberalism) in the face of the evidence, since it leads to despotism, via local the focus of a centralizing, Iberian state" (p. 396), for the configuration of his preference.

Victor Nunes Leal, in "Coronelismo, Enxada e Voto" agrees with Oliveira Viana that coronelism as an expression of the local leadership is not fruit of the structure politics, but rather a demonstration of how changes in structure (agrarian reform, for example) affect the intimacy of social relations and the representative and democratic order. For him, the rational legal order is compatible with the patrimonial order, having as consequence a representative democratic representation of the situation of "Cabresto" (1997, p. 56) of the vote (halting vote), linked to the patrimonial order. It is an in-depth work under the agrarian roots that exposes these insides as a product of the large farms integrated to the power of generalized form.

In his study, he takes into account the presence of the municipality, as well as the relationship with the other public powers of the country, state and federal. The basis of power comes, if not from property, at least from wealth.

If the local potentate does not have enough resources, he has no way to meet the needs of his friends, let alone the electoral expenses, which he often feels compelled to satisfy from his own pocket, although the creation of political parties has contributed to attenuate the sacrifices, through the party fund, formed with the subscriptions of the big firms, interested in maintaining good relations with the public powers: elections were always made with apportionment that took into account the number of regrouped votes.

Evaluating the micro level, from the municipality reports that from here comes the mentality of the vote, linking it to local patrimonialism. In fact, "state and federal politicians start there, carrying the same lack of idealism for the future, denoting factors that, although related to the personality of this subject, are closely related to our economic and social structure" (1997, p. 59).

It seems that, in this context, the author tries to explain the importance of the dependence of coronelism or localism in relation to the representative regime, showing as a "historical cut of changes of the criterion of the facade vote the revolution of 1930" (1997, p. 105), that in its constitution "seeks to rescue the lost dignity of the municipality". Even focusing on the municipality, a fundamental environment for its study on coronelism, defends centralism as a necessity of the servile regime. If the provinces were to have broad powers, it could happen that in some of them free labor ended slavery (1997, p. 97).

Therefore, centralizing to continue slavery would have defended the National Unity. As he delves into the role of colonelism in his work, emphasizing it as an instrument for strengthening public power in a decadent rural structure, he reports on the support he receives from the ruling party to ensure the stable predominance of a local political current (1997, p. 282).

Logically, the generation of this "immobilism" provided by the exchange of interests gives rise to the formation of opposition parties to this prevailing order.

On the role of the rulers, Thomas Skidmore points out in "Brazil: from Getúlio a Castelo" that Juscelino Kubitschek was little inclined to influence the existing rural property system that his label of nationalism was based on the Brazilian administrative and business elite and not on mass movements.

He explains that Kubitscheck made no attempt to mix left populism with developmental nationalism, "an act that was expected to unite middle class to the opposition military" (1969, p. 210).

Gaining the support of some intellectuals of nationalist ideas, attracted by faith in the future of Brazil and believers in the goodwill of its President to try to accelerate the process of economic change, ended up receiving from them, mainly through the ISEB, an awareness program and recruitment for his plan, which reached hundreds of student-years, reflecting on the reactive incapacity of the intellectuals of his radical left and opposition military, a difficulty further reinforced by the uncontested support of JK to his War Minister Lott maintain military support.

The Kubitschek Government later harvested the effects of mistreating the problem of rural property by witnessing the beginning of the radicalization of the countryside, encouraged by the populists of the left. In fact, according to Skidmore, "the signs of the political awakening of the masses in the urban and rural sectors would scare the groups that had more to lose if the balance of power were disturbed by the populists (1969, p. 207) never threatened", even in the populist phase of Vargas.

The urban middle class (which was still linked by various personal ties to the landowners, and was profoundly doubtful of its future condition in a period of rapid transformation) and the military class also revealed such signs; in the case of the military, with the peculiarity that their aversion to populism "stemmed from the fear of losing their position as supreme political arbiter, and partly because they disagreed on the proper strategy for Brazilian economic development" (1968, p. 227).

If Jânio Quadros maintained the same developmentalist tone, but also worried about external relations as a source of continuity of resources, he had less results in relation to his commitment. With his expansionist interests in Brazil, he brought the distrust of military men who observed their attempt to attain development by a "middle way between the West and Communism" (1968, p. 245).

The agrarian reforms that included the government proposal of João Goulart (called "Jango" from people) were defended in the conviction that an "archaic system of rural property prevented any increase of the agricultural production" (p.289). In this way, it was possible to argue that such reforms should be implemented urgently.

However, traditional landowners did not welcome the mobilization of rural masses that their government encouraged with the populist proposal. Like Jânio, conservative sectors of the armed forces denied support for the camp's Janguist (from "Jango") reform campaign.

The environment of the Agrarian Question from 45 to 64: the changes brought about by industrialization as a rural exodus in rural-urban relations

Industrialization already affirmed since before the 1950s, accompanied by a process of concentration of income with the integration of new Brazilian structures into the new post-war economic-capitalist order, leads to changes in field-city relations.

According to Linhares *et al.* (1990), the biggest of all the important changes of the period 1950-1980 is the inversion of the rural-urban relationship, where the rural population in 1950 represented 64% of the total population and the urban population 36%, passing in 1980, the first to 33% and the second to 67% of the total population. The economic axis thus shifts from the traditional and secular countryside of wealth production to cities, with the explosion of large cities such as São Paulo, Rio de Janeiro, and, on a smaller scale, some capitals that would concentrate around 30% of the entire Brazilian population (only in the Rio-São Paulo axis, 20%).

The exaggerated growth of these cities was due to the strong rural exodus that would cause destabilizing social conditions and predisposing the rural environment to a consequent increase of the violence, accompanied by a great increase of working population.

This contingent of workers was concentrated in the sectors of metallurgy, mechanics, electrical material, communications and transportation, with a marked decline in participation in sectors such as the textile and food industry.

But, in spite of the predominance and generalization of capitalist production relations, with the consequence of the urbanization of the country, "a non-capitalist sector, integrated and subsumed into the capitalist sector, composed of a myriad of workshops and manufactures in the cities, and a vast peasant contingent"(1990, p.303), will develop.

Discussions of this sector by Brazilian intellectuals and politicians were intense. In fact, all the archaic forms of credit to the old Brazilian agricultural vocation were being studied because of the barriers that came with industrial modernization.

In the discussions between the currents were, on the one hand, those who favored the traditional dualist-structural notion, where the feudalism/capitalism dichotomy was defended by liberals, "communists and ISEB reformers and, on the other hand, there was another generation of intellectuals such as Caio Prado Júnior or communists parties that wanted deeper transformations, from level to revolutionary change" (1990, p. 303).

In any case, in the sequence of the dialectical process, it was only a posteriori that this sector was absorbed by the logic of capital, without necessarily passing through the conventional relation of capitalist production, since it is not seen as eminently feudal.

If the non-feudal character of the history of Brazilian agriculture was the remnant of the series of discussions, the more lucid interpretations to understand the problem of the backwardness of the field led to a possibility that this non-linearized sector to the traditional relations of capitalist production could be "advanced" into a key role in the process of accumulation, acting as an input agent for industrialization.

The change of party mechanism in the composition of political forces

The relationship of imbalance shown in the field-city relations from the industrial boom of the fifties influenced decisively the partisan politics of the period and onwards, generating different expectations in conservative parties that start to receive the annoyances of the new ideas that surpass the agrarian-exporter-slave.

The Social Democratic Party (PSD), which had its main political base in the countryside, based on localism and colonelism, a system of voting control through economic coercion and coastal control, observed the decline of the rural population and the economic importance of the countryside.

In fact, the PSD feared, in particular, the advance of the Brazilian Labor Party (PTB) in rural areas, trying to expand its social base, hitherto restricted to the middle of urban workers, by extending social legislation to the countryside. On the other hand, the National Democratic Union (UDN) went through a similar crisis: routinely defeated in the majority elections by the PTB / PSD coalition, it was ready to turn to the military for its claims to expand its declining influence. Concern increased as the camp-city relationship increased the electorate of its main opponent: the PTB.

Teixeira da Silva together with Linhares (*op.cit.*,1990) analyzing the data of the TSE, comments on the jump from "the contingent of 7,459,849 voters in 1945 to 58,616,588 voters in 1982, at the same time that one could also see a sure decline of conservative parties in the set of valid votes, with the UDN from 27% of the total votes from 1945 to 13% in 1962 and the PSD from 44% to 18% in the same period "(1990, p. 306). On the contrary, the PTB enlarged its electorate and expanded to the interior, evidencing what General Golbery of Couto e Silva and lieutenant-colonel at the time, who was one of the students, a member of the permanent body and intelligence of the ESG, would have denominated as a "leftist-laborist" trend, well supported in industrialization and urbanization.

In this way, the political-partisan crisis progressed over the Armed Forces, where the legalism and opportunism of several senior officers positioned in a wing already explained as anti-nationalist-favored the injection of greater interference of US capital and political actions in Brazilian business-within the context of the Cold War, explicitly opposed Vargas and his Labor.

The episode of the increase of 100% of the minimum wage, among other populist measures of the last government of Vargas, was considered by this military chain as good opportunities of conspiracy against him, forcing the resignation of João Goulart, his minister of labor and his executor of his view of a "syndicalist republic", as shown.

If the resignation did not occur, with Vargas' suicide, the syndicalist dream seems to have been an expression of the governmental reality of João Goulart, who ends up accumulating even more military enemies in politics when he attempts to subvert the unity of the military institution in the call of the sergeants against the officers, in the "Automobile Club of Brazil" episode, the moment when the 1964 force regime began.

Victory in the Military Club benefited the opposition wing of Vargas's populist policy, which reinforces the UDN's political participation in Armed forces. Juarez Távora in 1955 is launched by this legend as presidential candidate, but was defeated by the PSD/PTB coalition that came with Juscelino Kubitschek and João Goulart as president and vice president, respectively.

The conspiracy continued because of the disappointment of the anti-nationalist military wing that creates to use the physical and symbolic extinction of Vargas as forms of seizure of the power.

The future putschists of 1964, an armed and industrial arm linked to capitalist production relations, signed in a military-techno-bureaucratic alliance, induce Café Filho to unite with the industrial member of the system, represented by Eugênio Gudin and Eduardo Gomes as candidate of the UDN to fight Kubstichek before his inauguration. Colonel Jurandyr of Bizarria Mamede of the permanent body of the ESG publicly defies the nationalist general Henrique Teixeira Lott (minister of war) and, a supporter of legalism in the Armed Forces and Labor. Café Filho did not want to punish the colonel, allowing a crisis of insubordination to appear in the army's folder.

The Minister of War could not directly punish Colonel Mamede, as the military was subordinate to the ESG and the school escaped the jurisdiction of the army brief, since ESG is an educational establishment subordinate to the Joint Chiefs of Staff. Faced with such a crisis, Café Filho is forced to resign for "health reasons".

The mayor, Carlos Luz, assumes the presidency maintaining the same political line of Café Filho, displeasing Lott. This, feeling wronged in his convictions and his authority, forces the preventive blow of November 11, 1955, where he assumes Nereu Ramos, president of the Brazilian Senate and who protects the possession of Kubstichek and João Goulart ("JK" and "Jango").

The anti-nationalist current of the Armed Forces in its campaign of ideologization attempted to unify the military currents, which was allowed, despite the developmentalism accompanied by Juscelino Kubitschek (who was also accused of mismanaging the country's finances in such a growth expensive and inflationary program) was favorable to the expansion of political-military influence.

If the discrediting of "JK" was already greater, it is necessary to consider the influence of the ISEB in the plan of goals of its government that was favorable to the capitalist modernization, but located in a form opposite to the block of the ESG regarding the ideological option. Jânio Quadros, UDN candidate, under the augury of economic recovery and austerity, well remembered for the "broomstick" he usually carried to characterize his interest in political and economic sanitation, does not demonstrate either to conjugate well the military forces in the party that elected him and which had strong conservative representation of the Armed Forces.

In addition, João Goulart was again elected as vice president and the PTB, along with the PSD, already had strong congressional seats. Superior wear and tear led him to accentuate the crises with the Armed Forces that had not yet withdrawn him from his project because of the representative and partisan influence he had.

The ruling classes, cultural elites, and military leaders formed under the direct influence of the US Command and Staff College, the US National War College or the American School of the Americas, among other doctrinal training establishments within the Cold War knew of the progress, increasingly, of the Brazilian left and they saw the hopes of democratically preventing the rise of labor reformism to power.

In this way, it is possible to better understand the UDN's call for military coup, apologizing for the personal flaws of Jânio Quadros or João Goulart in this understanding.

The great Agrarian Reform project and the resistance: 1945-1964

The establishment of a Nationalist Parliamentary Front to realize the outline of the centrist wing of the PTB also showed the internal dissidents of this great party. The dilution of its influence would be vital for the non-ruralist military apparatus and lacking in its representativeness. Thus, Santiago Dantas and Hermes Lima, supporters of the center of this party, who were sometimes invited to give lectures at ESG, were in favor of continuing the alliance with the PSD and the moderate reforms through the "Basic Reforms" plan of João Goulart.

In general terms, this proposed modernism explored very nationalistic, pro-statist characteristics, but it could not be understood as a socialist party, as Teixeira da Silva points out (Linhares *et al.*,Op. cit., 1990).

The main idea of its platform was to overcome backwardness and poverty, both generated by the capitalist-mercantilist environment. Within their most extreme internal tendencies, however, it was possible to verify the origin of these ideas through the analysis of what was proposed by the Third Socialist International, which said that backward and underdeveloped countries should unite their popular classes, since by numerical and structural weakness of the industrial proletariat, it would be unable to carry out the revolution alone (or profound reform).

This model would have already reached the PTB in two ways: communist, since the 1947 lawlessness and through analyzes of the ISEB, also linked to some communist matrices. Nelson Werneck Sodré, one of ISEB's military professors, does not believe that the *bourgeoisie* could carry out the reforms necessary for the development of the country without the movement of all classes.

The task, according to Teixeira da Silva (Linhares *et al.*,Op. cit., 1990, p. 310), would be a vast "set comprising the peasantry, the petty bourgeoisie and parts of the upper and middle bourgeoisie," which was clearly contrary to the anti-nationalist military view that condition of communist subversion.

Thus, the struggle defended by Juscelino Kubstichek (although his orientation at the beginning of his administration on corporate mergers motivated an advance in Brazil-US relations) could unite these segments in a proposal that did not accept submission to the which would be the colonial inheritance, of dependence on the foreigner coming from a new American and "democratic" dress.

Technically, according to Teixeira da Silva, the strong land concentration from more than three centuries of colonial dependence, had characterized the process of expansion of large estates and expulsion of the rural worker, despite the industrial development, outlining the period of 1945 to 1964.

In the analysis of the problem, Teixeira da Silva tells us that the 1960 census provides important material for the understanding of the Brazilian agrarian question, noting that Brazilian territory was effectively occupied in only 31%, divided into 3,350,000 characterized in three groups of analysis:

In the first group, there were small properties (less than 100 hectares): within this group were small farms (with approximately 10 hectares) originating, for the most part, the sharing of family properties, comprising a universe of more than 700 thousand properties, which ranged from under-utilization, due to credit and financing difficulties, to intense exploitation aimed at keeping a population disproportionate to its potential; the farms, from 10 to 50 hectares, representing 36.5% of the properties, 10.8% of the total area and 32.3% of the cultivated area of the country; and the sites, from 50 to 100 hectares, with extensive use of non-family labor, unlike previous units.

These companies would then be responsible for the supply of labor for the industrialization process, supplying the domestic market, often producing much greater productivity than that of large estates, making up the main core of temporary plantations; in total, sites and farms accounted for 44.6% of the properties in 1960, covering 17.9% of the appropriate area, contributing 44.7% of the cultivated area and absorbing about 50% of the rural labor force.

Such would have profoundly "influenced Celso Furtado and other thinkers who visualized the Brazilian projection in the post-1960s and who viewed agrarian reform as an unlocking of the economy and, at the same time, an immense step towards the efficiency and rationalization of agricultural production, in an accelerated industrialization phase". Diagnosis implied the multiplication of the private property of the land and in no way resembled a collectivist project (1990, p. 311)

Secondly, medium-sized farms (commercial farms), which were properties from 100 to 1000 hectares, represented 9.5% of the properties, dominating, however 32.5% of the area registered.

It was characterized by the great investment of capital and a high degree of commercialization, giving the market a high proportion of its total production and by the regular use of salaried labor.

Thirdly, the large farms: with more than 1000 hectares of area, varying, however, of region, representing 0.9% of the properties, occupying, however 47% of the total land, cultivating only 2.3% of this area, contributing only 11.5% of production and occupying 7% of the active rural labor force.

Most large farms were unproductive, with natural pastures occupying 60% of the pastures, although responding with only 36.6% of the cattle herd or renting land to third parties, as in the areas of triticulture and rhiziculture in the south of the country or of cotton and peanuts in São Paulo.

Since 1961, with the resurgence of the supply crisis and a high rate of inflationary growth, the government is pressed for a quick and effective response to the agrarian question, which was forcing the industrialization project.

The Statute of the Rural Worker (1963) would have been the first great step towards the solution of the political-economic problem. At its core were Vargas' labor ideas accumulated by years of John Goulart's experience alongside his dynamics.

The Statute also allowed the extension of the social legislation and the diversification of trade unions to the field, not only to the urban environment. Ensuring the minimum wage for the eight-hour days, among other social security benefits of the Italian *Carta di Lavoro* model used by Getulio Vargas, would lead the agrarian environment to enter into the content of capitalist production relations. But the Statute produced social burdens that would not be borne by the big landowners, a fact that led to the expulsion of many workers.

João Goulart, in the Triennial Plan for Economic and Social Development (1963-1965) already accentuated the reformist pressures on the large landowners, since it provided that there would be immunity from payment of income over economically used land for the worker who, during a full agricultural cycle, had occupied virgin lands and remained uncontested in them. In addition, it guaranteed lands for the agricultural worker, tenant or tenant who was for two or more years in a property.

And, worst of all, for farmers, he asked for the expropriation of all lands necessary for food production, with payment expected for the long term.

Two weeks before March 31, 1964, João Goulart sent to Congress a large agrarian reform project cannot be voted.

All the initiatives to unlock the economy studied by the group of intellectuals of this decade and embodied in the Agrarian Reform project were harshly accused of "communist" content and incisively condemned by the party center and right, especially the PSD, with strong rural representation in Minas Gerais and in the Northeast, sites of historic congregation of local political colonels based on the large agrarian-exporting property of the colonial monopoly that used access to land as an element of electoral bargaining.

The agrarian reform from the point of view of party logic was what diverted the PTB of the PSD at that moment, causing the PSD to join the UDN, traditional opponent of Vargas, Goulart and Brizola. Another element that makes up this precious picture is the agitation that took place in the Northeast when reclamations by land and a popular initiative for the deconcentration of lands in the hands of the traditional landowners, are now seen as "police cases."

And in 1955, the Agricultural and Livestock Society of Planters, known as Peasant Leagues, led by Francisco Julião, became the center of popular mobilization in the countryside, a point of support for Goulart, Miguel Arraes and others, as well as the heart of hysteria anticommunist.

The 1946 Constitution, which had a strong liberal content after the removal of Vargas, was not effective in signaling the real reforms intended by the Nationalist Parliamentary Front, since land redistribution was impossible by its § 16 of Article 141 (of the Federal Constitution of 1946) that demanded the payment of compensation "just and prior, in cash, for the expropriations of public interest".

The UDN had participated with a majority of this constitution that would preserve the private economic order. But, in fact, the growing force of popular mobilization was appearing in the Cold War environment, where the rhetoric of a free and capitalist world as well as the focal point of the Cuban Revolution was the land issue. This passed to the Brazilian agrarian population in the idea that the land did not have to be the exclusive patrimony of those who always owned it.

Considering the condition of exclusion for almost the entire national history, the popular masses would serve as a fopp and beautiful arrangement for communism to organize the collectivization of the country. In this case, the duality of the ideological dispute over the economic model that suited him best, could, for the communist side inspired by the Cuban vision, came accompanied by criticism of the principle of private property that was being threatened.

In fact, this was an important alignment item with the US, as several American companies already installed in the country saw possibilities of using land as a reserve of value, which was well shown in the post-64 when the growing demand for products priests led large foreign holdings or groups to explore their businesses from vacant or expropriated lands.

Thus, Teixeira da Silva points out that "the agrarian reform issue became even more tense since it involved large international capital and national companies whose agricultural sector was not at times dominant in business activity and which", (1990, p. 315).

In Goulart's time, however, the central question was in the understanding that industrialization needed an agrarian reform that would guarantee an end to inflation, low wages and abundance of raw materials, through agricultural modernization and the overcoming of traditional, backward and unproductive large farms.

The impatience of the popular leaders with Goulart's impotence in front of Congress and the institutional barriers to continue agrarian reform proclaimed a series of agrarian pro-reform protests to outrance, leading authorities of state violence to position themselves.

General Artur da Costa e Silva, then military commander of the Fourth Army (Northeast), orders the repression of the peasants' leaders, who were ordered by landlords. The depression leads to the paralysis of private investments, accentuating the overthrow of Goulart.

In addition, his independent foreign policy led by Santiago Dantas prevented the flow of American capital. Kennedy tried several times to seek an alignment of foreign policies, but he could not hide the real American pretension of impeding the "communist" advance in Brazil through the submission of foreign policy. He granted local resources for the problem of hunger in the Northeast (there he was, with the Peasant Leagues the main insurrectional focus), contenting some and displeasing others, since he channeled them to the political battle of the ballot box against Goulart, or to those against him. Kennedy donates great resources to the Brazilian Institute for Democratic Action (IBAD) and the Institute for Research and Social Studies (IPES). These institutes started to have a common political action with the advice of the intelligence of the ESG and ended up assuming the financial support of the campaign for the defense of the foreign capital and against the agrarian reform.

The blockade of Cuba served to intensify the American mood and large sums of the Central Intelligence Agency (CIA) accelerated the opposition campaign.

The consequence of the 1964 coup ended Goulart's agrarian reform policy, opening space for studies adaptive to the new policy of regulation of usufruct and land ownership with the Castelo Branco Land Statute.

Agricultural modernization, the 1950s and ESG: classification of agrarian categories: natural resources in the ESG doctrine

The updating of the summary of the ESG doctrine, due to new conjunctures and actions, characterizes its flexibility to meet the varied requests for studies to guide political action.

Thus, the entry of the study of agriculture, agriculture, fishing or related are framed in a similar place for didactic purposes.

By doctrine, national power is divided into expressions of power, and expressions are subdivided into categories of analysis. For the understanding of the characterizations we see what "national power" is for ESG[55]:

> (...) National Power is the capacity that has the interacting set of the men and the means that constitute the Nation, acting in conformity of the national will, to achieve and to maintain the National Goals (...)

In the text there is an unfolding that is bold. The understanding of "national objectives", according to the brochure "Doctrinal Foundations of ESG" (1997, p. 37), follows:

> (...) National Objectives (ON) are the crystallization of necessities, interests and aspirations, vital or optional, that at a certain stage of their historical-cultural evolution, the Nation seeks to satisfy (...)

But the economic expression of national power, also made explicit in this brochure (1997, p. 79), needs to be defined:

> (...) Economic Expression of National Power is the predominantly economic manifestation of the interactive set of men and the means that constitute the National Power, in order to achieve and preserve the National Objectives.

---

[55] See *Fundamentos Doutrinários da Escola Superior de Guerra*. Rio de Janeiro: A Escola, 1997, p.49.

Within the classification encompassed by this economic expression of power lies the topic of natural resources, which constitute the patrimonial assets of the country. ESG refers to these resources as one of the components of "manifestation of the Foundations of National Power in Economic Expression" (p.80), alongside Human Resources and Economic Institutions.

The vision of exploitation of the natural resources of the ESG is connected to the sense of appropriation for the usufruct of the productive forces. Despite commenting on the "conservationist" practices of these resources that should be recommended, it strongly aligns with the logic of the market, commenting on the dynamism of the global relationships that are characterized by competition or conflict. Thus, through the brochure (1997, p. 83), he understands that the "changes in socio-economic behavior" resulting from this type of approach has the following characteristics:

1) the economy's recovery through the expansion of the market;

2) the restructuring of power centers through the formation of megablocks with direct influence on the markets; and

3) new and different patterns of production, organization and business administration, as well as deepening the discussion about the role of the state in the economy.

When speaking of Economic Institutions, the generalist approach initially prejudices the analysis, since it considers that they "have a preponderant role in promoting or limiting development" (p. 84), but then instructs that the assurance these Institutions present in development effort must be pursued.

It considers the economic system as one of those institutions that would involve the market, the company, the consumption, the currency and its unfolding. If market relations and national power are always interconnected in their actions, it is necessary to verify what the School understands by economic factors:

(...) They are elements capable of producing quantitative and qualitative variations in the foundations of National Power and in all components of the Economic System, as well as in the relations between them, in order to produce economic effects (p.84).

Thus, productive and entrepreneurial capacity, observed from the institution-enterprise perspective, the scientific and technological capacity, which increases industrial and collective productivity, and propitiates productivity gains, are aspects present in the definition of these economic factors.

4 THE ANALYSIS OF THE MONOGRAPHS PRODUCED IN ESG

Agricultural production and technical rigor in ESG

The discussions about the development of ESG's work are divided between faculty and students. In its own educational methodological approach, ESG students prepare documents within the School's doctrine with a precondition.

This precondition is provided through lectures, sensitization, study visits and group work with the accompaniment of faculty members or "connections", graduates of the ESG who are able to guide the students in the conduct of the doctrine, aiming at a productivity of quality.

In this way, we will begin to uncover some of the documents selected for the discussion of the problem.

The first document registered in the ESG on the Agrarian Question is from the very year of its foundation.

This document is organized in a collection that covers the topic of "Agriculture and Livestock", spelled out in a series of two separate titles and two lecturers. Álvaro Barcelos Fagundes[56] will also be invited the following year to talk about "agricultural production", theme of his talk in 1950.

From his conference in the year 49[57], one can verify: 1) a concern with the characterization environment, climate and soil physiographic; 2) the delimitation of the extractive activity in the country, circumscribed to phytogeographic characteristics: cocais area, caatingas zone, coastal forest zone, pine forest zone, field zone and maritime zone; 3) a "passage" over the pastoral industry in which it categorizes and counts the herds in Brazil and 4) agricultural production, disseminated by traditional export monocultures.

---

[56] Agronomist of the Ministry of Agriculture. Director of the National Agronomic Research Service. He held the position of Director of the Institute of Agricultural Experimentation. He was the representative of Brazil at the Wheat Conferences in London and conservation of Natural Resources in Uruguay. He had been a regular ESG lecturer since 1949

[57] Under the document of the ESG: A-014, 016-49-*Agricultura e Pecuária*.

From the conclusions that one identifies about the agricultural production, when it analyzes the period of 1930/1948 is that it emphasizes the productive decrease of the coffee, like unique product in these conditions. Cotton production increased from 1930/1944 to 1944/1948, although the volume produced in 1948 was equivalent to three times what it was produced in 1930. Corn production fluctuates a lot, mentioning that in 1948 it was 12% above of the level of 1930. Other crops of rice, sugar cane, manioc, beans, potatoes, wheat and cacao maintained regularity in the production curve[58].

When he talks about agricultural production in 1950[59], Álvaro explains the details of using the technique to better explore the soil. He considers one of the indispensable requirements for the establishment of agriculture as a permanent and profitable activity the use of adequate techniques and means to assure a low cost of production.

He analyzes the soil fertility problems, showing the requirements of the superior plants and their peculiarities in relation to fertilization, the reaction of the soil to the needs of fertilization and the definition of the main nutrients of the soil. In the conclusions of his work, he shows that it is essential to: 1) disseminate among farmers the concept of need for fertilization and its importance, to raise crop yields and, consequently, to lower the cost of production; 2) develop the fertilizer and corrective industry; 3) stimulate the importation of fertilizer materials and 4) facilitate and cheapen means of transportation of fertilizers and correctives.

The technical content that was being seen in these studies was tied to the serious gender supply crisis (and the example of declining Coffee is an account of its loss of acceptance as an export product, but also indicative of an avant-garde proposal of industrialization) stemming from a weak land structure that severely damaged the amount of Brazilian exports of agricultural products and the Brazilian trade balance, but was rooted in the interventionist state policy of 1930, which had become interested in political-administrative reorganization, the supply problem.

If social classes had not been structured into divisions of labor, according to the classic English-business bourgeoisie / agrarian aristocracy and industrial classes-the sharp rural exodus and the formation of a potential industrial reserve army would permit the union of sectors of the industrial *bourgeoisie*, military and urban labor.

In addition, with the II WW, the inevitable politicization by the hegemonic blocs arrives in Brazil and is accompanied by the military antinationalist chain as, beyond a mere subordination to the American interests, strategic possibility of reconstruction of the Brazilian capacity, definitively freed from the economic-historical link European geography and anti-colonial struggles.

The study of the alternatives of monocultures to compensate for the deficiency of food and the search for the balance of the land structure was well seen by the ESG doctrine and necessary to the satisfactory performance of the exercise of National Power through its economic expression.

Otherwise, ESG students, in order to carry out their work, needed this multivision of national problems and studies on the Brazilian agricultural vocation or the relations of capitalist production in the countryside were also made by Brazilian society.

---

[58] It uses as source the Production Statistics Service of the Ministry of Agriculture. The lecturer says that the same table on agricultural production from 1944-1948 had been presented by the then Minister of Agriculture-Daniel de Carvalho at a conference at the Army's School of General Staff.

[59] ESG document A-002-50-*Produção Agrícola*

Another lecturer, the Minister of Agriculture in 1952, João Cleofas de Oliveira[60], talks about the national agrarian policy at the invitation of the then commander of ESG-General Cordeiro de Farias and, at the outset, talks about the serious problem of production and subsistence, who would have transmitted to Getúlio Vargas: "To confront this situation, it is a force to confess, Your Excellency, the Ministry of Agriculture is completely disappeared ..." (1952, p. 02).

Used that in order to base his ideas on the listeners, because since two decades before had occurred common verifications of capital investment previously applied to large export agriculture, who are motivated by the lack of courage with the problem of coffee prices, and which would corroborate discouragement of all Brazilian agricultural production.

Defending agriculture, he mentions that "excluding the east, Brazil is one of the countries with the highest proportion of people employed in agriculture."

Obviously, the lack of an agricultural framework affects the safety of the industry, as a result of the transformation of farm goods into an instrument of internal consumption, not merely an external one; an interesting phenomenon of land concentration, compounded by the technical and financial incapacity faced by farmers who, not receiving adequate assistance from the public authorities, seek the "humus of the virgin lands" and cease to be grounded, benefiting well exploring it (p.5). In his reasoning, it shows the attack of speculators who exploit the unused lands and that keeps the unproductive lands waiting for the valorization real estate.

This is the record of the "lack of means" (p. 7) for agricultural development. How can we have a progressive, rationalist agricultural farmer interested in his technical improvement if the problems of agricultural credit, technical assistance and mechanization of agriculture are not a priority?

At that moment, the mechanization tonic becomes important so that the old techniques of management, with rudimentary artifacts, used in subsistence are replaced by those most effective for the logic of capitalist production relations. "Tractor hunger"[61] is a solution for the increase of rural wages and industrial progress, based on these inputs produced by a specialized contingent of workers who would escape from the economic flight to the cities, besides allowing the development of basic agricultural production by increasing the individual productive capacity of the farmer.

From technicalism to the proposals of agrarian structural reform: 1955-1960

Among the works of the selected students is that of João Kessler Coelho de Souza[62] who despite having received the guidance of the ESG in a reserved document cataloged as E 04-55 to present the monograph under the title of Agriculture and Raw Materials Vegetable demonstrates his excuse to the performance minor, for his ineptitude: a non-specialist of the subject (p.1).

---

[60] Also Civil Engineer, formed by the former Polytechnic School of Rio de Janeiro. He was mayor of Vitória-ES, State Representative and Secretary of Agriculture of the State of Pernambuco. ESG regular lecturer. ESG Doc A-012-52-*Política Agrária Nacional*

[61] The first plan of mechanization of agriculture was made in 1943 (II Vargas government) in the administration of the Minister of Agriculture Apolônio Sales, with the goal of competing for the effort of the II GM, motivated also by the influence of the American industrial park.

[62] Doc ESG T-29-55-*Agricultura e Matérias Primas Vegetais.*

However, if Kessler says not to develop according to the depth required by the ESG, he joins another document developed by a group of agricultural studies of the ESG, among other reports related to the Third Brazilian Rural Conference[63] held in São Paulo in December 1954 and that it considers important in its research, since it is document cataloged in the bibliography recommended by the ESG for the Work.

As for the document written by ESG students, Task Group G-09-55[64], in charge of the study of the "national economic situation" aiming at increasing productivity in the agricultural and industrial sectors, separates the main topics.

In this work, there is immediately a critique of the mechanization of the land as a fad, since modernization depends initially on the fertilization of the soil for its effectiveness.

Poor soils may be useful to the exploitation if properly nitrogenated and document points out as necessary the mapping of all types of soil for fertilization, through the belief that fertilization of these soils is one of the main factors of agricultural production (pp.41- 42).

The document also points out the other factors of low agricultural productivity: a) illiteracy of rural man (70-80%); b) poor sanitary conditions in rural areas; c) the lack of significant technical assistance; d) the ingrained routine of devastation and burning, followed by abandonment of land; (e) excessive use of low-income labor; f) the use of generally unselected and immunized seeds; (g) lack of storage in production, distribution and consumption areas; (h) a lack of regular transport, often leading to the loss of a large proportion of production or at least delays in making it available to markets; and (i) the lack of improved techniques applied to tropical crops (p.44).

The soils that characterize low fertility end up interfering decisively in the index of agricultural productivity, namely: 1) Amazon region; 2) caatingas of the Northeast; 3) closed from the central plateau. In this way, it points to an unbalanced global growth in agricultural production due to the dispersion of crops and large amounts of low-fertility soils.

Finally, the document (p.51) establishes the "lines of action" for agriculture of the period, which suggest the organization of agriculture in order to harmonize with the industrialization project, which should aid in its development.

These suggestions of the group are organized according to the doctrinal method of the School and separated by the "field" of Power, which are in reality the characterization of the analysis of the commitment of the problem, separated from the "national power". (pp.52-54)

1) In the administrative field;

(a) to finance cooperatives and rural associations, the establishment of a network of warehouses in the areas of production, distribution and consumption, in order to reduce waste and regulate the flow of production; ensure the agriculture of the land it needs, preventing the rise of its prices to prohibitive limits of activity;

(b) as a result of the increase in the cargo to be transported: to encourage the supply of local resources, to re-equip the merchant marine by providing it with ships suitable for the products to be transported and to retrofit the railways with the same gauge.

---

[63] Full conference reports are available in the appendix of pages 97-151 from doc above.
[64] Your members could not be identified.

<u>2)</u> In the technological field:

(a) guide the producer in the operation of crops with the best ecological adaptation;

b) to encourage the establishment of fertilizer industries, granting them advantages that can lower the prices of these products in order to allow the intensive use of corrections and fertilizers by farmers to complement the existing fertility factors in the soils in operation;

c) increase the number of existing experimental stations for the diffusion of agricultural technique in general and adequate soil nitrogenization;

d) to combat pests and rodents that attack crops;

e) distribute seeds, seedlings, etc., from specimens of high productivity, resistant to climatic adversities and,

f) encourage the equipping of agricultural properties with material appropriate to the respective types of exploitation.

<u>3)</u> In the psychosocial field:

a) to develop a campaign to attract more young people to the study of agricultural and livestock techniques in their various types and stages of complexity.

b) to preach, in full, the need for producers to adopt new methods and techniques capable of increasing productivity, showing them how much they will benefit from much more rewarding profits.

<u>4)</u> In the camp the creation of a rational and definitive system of rural credit, the only means capable of providing, on a high scale, an increase in agricultural productivity, due to the lack of capital and technique. Rural credit expansion would allow the boost to production, a reorganization of transport and a new demand for markets. It is suggested, for the conquest of new markets abroad, the replacement of the current commercial offices of the Ministry of Labor abroad by Chambers of Commerce, which are obliged to maintain permanent fairs of Brazilian products.

This context of propositions of structural modifications was closely related to the problem also accentuated from the 1930s, in the analysis of Teixeira da Silva (1981, p. 39):

1) from the external point of view, "the strengthening of American capitalism and its new forms of intervention under direct investments in industry; loans and technical cooperation; purchase of national companies already installed and diversification of the economic and financial sphere, besides the military aid provided by the Brazil-US Military Agreement";

2) from the internal point of view, "the trend of accentuation of income concentration, inflation, falling wages, fall in the rate of accumulation of the industrial sector, deterioration of terms of trade and its consequence of the scarcity of foreign exchange", which led to a expansion of the domestic market or re-equipping the park with the introduction of foreign capital.

As for this impasse, the expansion of domestic markets would lead to a need for fundamental socio-political support for the movement to change structures. Already, the idea of the re-equipping of the Brazilian park by the American resources, as a matter of priority, would be an option to rearticulate the classes and social and economic groups linked to the interests of "denationalization".

The work of group TG-13-56[65] received the reserved mission of "based on the

---

[65] The work was recommended by the Head of the Economic Affairs Division of ESG, Air Force Colonel

National Strategic Concept and through an objective and accurate examination of the national and international conjuncture and the direction and pace of its foreseeable evolution, to analyze, from the point of view agricultural industrialization as follows:

a) its repercussion in the economy;

b) social welfare, particularly the improvement of living standards in the various regions considered;

c) increasing the productivity of human potential used in farming;

d) work on the various missions and commissions;

e) suggest measures capable of remedying, in the shortest possible time, the identified deficiencies ".

During this period, according to Otavio Guilherme Velho (Velho, 1976), who had made a short transition since the death of Vargas until the arrival of Juscelino Kubitschek, "there were attempts to eliminate the" exchange confiscation "that allowed the transfer of capital from agriculture to industry and to impose a severe monetarist policy that would lower production levels." (p.162).

When Kubitschek took office, the country was practically self-sufficient in light consumer goods. Industrialization focused on durable consumer goods and capital goods. This required more capital and more sophisticated technology.

Being part of an uneven and combined development, this capital and technology would not normally be provided by internal sources, since this would mean retaking steps already taken by capitalist development on a world scale. In this way, the Kubitschek period saw a crucial turn in the direction of foreign investors, who were given special incentives (1976, p. 163).

In this context, the TG 13-56 effort reinforced the close relationship between agricultural development and industry. Historically, the English industrial outbreak disproportionate to agricultural possibilities, led to dependence on external supplies, in this case, the Commonwealth. But, unfortunately, Brazil had also been a colony, and such an appeal was not admissible.

Therefore, the agricultural-industry exchange propositions should come under the label of industrialization of agricultural products and not through the increase in extractive activity. But, in what way? a certain "cosmopolitanism", in the words of Otávio Velho (Velho, 1976, p.163), led to the dubiousness of expanding the internal market with inputs from the base industry raised with foreign capital.

In this movement, "TG" points to the advantages of the industrialization of agricultural products: a) dispenses the task of elaboration, preparation for consumption, leading to an economy of human means in the collection, selection, packing and sending; b) exempts the use of capital in processing facilities in the rural property; c) value the production, which benefits from organizations of superior equipment and specialized technique, becomes standardized derivatives of the best quality and without waste; d) it stimulates the intensification of the specialized production, by the greater yield that it makes possible; and, e) expands the scope of commercialization of production, with all the advantages for the market (TG 13-56, p.19).

When addressing the "well-being" of the agrarian population, when it undergoes a

---

Oswaldo Balloussier for publication. It was constituted by a Brigadier, three superior officers, a former minister of State, among its members. See p.2

pro-development effort in the field, it shows its concern with studies that point, as of 1948, to the waste of agricultural production, the lack of industrialization. In defense of the agrarian economy, he exhorts the elimination of the heavy losses and the "inhuman sacrifice of so many obscure workers on the farm, who are improperly exhausted, in the primitivism of the processes of elaboration of their raw material" (TG 13-56, p. 29).

The guidelines of the mission given by the ESG oblige the elaboration of its improve the picture. The group suggests an immediate action of "development plans" [66] of the production, in order to increase the export index of "106 articles that the world buys to us, industrializing all those that can compete in the market with the foreign counterparts" (TG 13-56, p.37).

It forecasts a rise in the value of our agricultural exports to the order of US $ 2,000,000,000.00 / Year, which could give rise to conditions of Brazilian independence in the sector, increasing economic power. Although it does not show how to do this, it continues to make general suggestions.

Among the main suggestions are the encouragement of a banking credit policy for agriculture, the technical improvement necessary for the changes, the donation of an exchange system to stimulate agricultural production and development, the adequacy of the main technical advisory services and considers the particular importance for National Security of the development of agricultural activities in the North and Northeast, providing a broader means to the agronomic institutes located there, so as to accelerate the necessary scientific research to progress the agricultural exploitation in these regions.

A conservative dualist conception[67] that ran to the time theorized about the interpretation of economic and social structures not only of Brazil, but of countries of colonial past. The duality he proposed was in the division of an open and modern sector and a closed and archaic sector. The modern was linked to industry, to large commerce, and to archaic, to the immobility of the interior, reminiscent of large farms, of useless population, unemployed and dependent on the paternalism of their employers.

In logic, it would be up to the modern to overcome the resistances of the archaic, offering him capitals, techniques, progress. For this dualism, the resistance to changes of the interior would be placed in the large farms of feudal nature, hierarchized from the social point of view and that would tend to fix the man to the earth. If man is usually attached to the land, one thinks of the possibility of encouraging his productivity there, but not of offering it, so that the relations of production would not be affected.

The interesting question of differentiation of this dualist thesis in relation to others lies in the emphasis given to the geophysiological conditions of the interior areas and to the mentality of the inhabitants, definitely against the relations of production. For this model of analysis, the modification of the land structure was not fundamental to the development of capitalism in Brazil.

---

[66] The ESG in its doctrine also draws up plans. It is not without nexus that National Development Plans were used in the decades of the Military Regime. In the Method of Planning for Policy Action, in its strategic phase, one learns to plan in levels of direction. Until now (see Fundamentos Doutrinários da ESG-1997, pp. 235-240), the exercise of the elaboration of Government Plans is observed.

[67] LAMBERT, Jacques, *Os Dois Brasis*, Rio de Janeiro, INEP, Centro Brasileiro de Pesquisas Educacionais, 1959. BASTIDE, Roger. *Brasil, Terra de Contrastes*, São Paulo, Difusão Européia do Livro, 1973.

Consequently, agrarian reform, by the access of the direct producers of the land, was inadvisable. Moreover, rather than the extensive redistribution of land, it was a question of increasing agricultural productivity through technological modernization and the reorganization of production by the grouping of properties into large capitalist cooperatives.

Another factor, that of the mentality of the Brazilian capitalists, prevented saving and productive investment, thus requiring the participation of foreign capital. Then nationalism was seen as harmful, since it distrusted foreign contribution. This last factor was strongly defended by the anti-nationalist wing, in the discussions already seen in the Military Club.

Later, when Celso Furtado[68] deepens the solutions for the backwardness of the countryside, he ends up changing the dualistic proposition cited, since through political, social, and finally structural reforms, unproductive areas and their inhabitants could be used in the development process.

The first class work of José Emilio Gonçalves Araújo's ESG, cataloged as TT1-27-57[69], attempts to raise the "effective national potential" of agriculture in 1957. It is a complex, drafted work and developed by a specialist who elaborates a complete summary of the Brazilian agrarian panorama, within a perspective of analysis that goes from the context of agriculture in the national economy, through the effective agricultural production in Brazil, the search for better productivity, the relations between agriculture and industry, rural exodus, agricultural education from the technical level to the top in the preparation of the researcher by the Rural University and abroad; finalizing by the formulation of ideas for an agrarian policy.

He argues that analyzes made in 1956 would have shown that the Brazilian rural production - agricultural, extractive plant and animal - would point to a relative amount of 30.3% of the National Income formation.

In development, rural activities would be the most important, if analyzed separately for the increase of the National Income. Of this total, agricultural activities, especially 16 crops in 1956: coffee, rice, maize, cotton, beans, cane, wheat, cassava, potatoes, cacao, bananas, orange, tobacco, cottonseed, grapes and sweet potatoes, would account for about 73%.

Despite the condition that stands out in favor of these important crops in Brazilian agriculture, he emphasizes the regional inequalities, the poor distribution of the agricultural production distribution, responsible for the inequality of economic power in the various physiographic areas[70]. He highlights the highly responsible role of

---

[68] He creates the discussion with the publication of the Brazilian Economic Formation that makes him famous. Celso F. served the governments of JK and João Goulart as one of the mentors of SUDENE (Northeast Development Planner and Executer), who had tested many of his ideas. The military anti-nationalist wing, however, linked its reformist actions to subversive possibilities, mainly because the reformist initiatives aligned themselves with the projects of João Goulart, in that environment of the Cold War. Furtado had a past of socialist militant when young and, finally, this was used against him in the vicinity of the force regime of 64, losing the oversight. Furtado, in his administration, fought hard against the oligarchies, but in my view, it was an anachronistic struggle for the setbacks he suffered. See an autobiography in his book "A Operação Nordeste".

[69] Full Professor of Agricultural Geology, School of Agronomy Eliseu Maciel, IAS / SNPA / CNEPA, Ministry of Agriculture.

[70] Professor Emílio presents the tabulation of the agricultural production of 1952-56 of all the Units of the

the coffee, cotton and cocoa crops that represent the country's basic export. The decline in coffee is also marked by its lower quality than other exporting countries, despite representing 50% of world production.

In fact, the coffee sector had provided from 1947 to 1954 the foreign exchange base necessary for the expansion and modernization of the industrial capital stock in the first phase of the post-war import substitution process[71].

Bouncing the perspective, the internalization of cultures, the expansion of new frontiers-Paraná in the 1940s and the Midwest and the Amazon from the 1960s, no doubt explains the longevity of the extensive model and the secondary importance attributed by the leaders to programs intended to accelerate the increase in production. Thus, the incorporation of new farmland accounted for 92% of the overall production increase in the period 1948-69[72].

Despite this, the expansion of cultivated area is also the main component of the growth of 22 sectors of agricultural products in all States, except for Rio de Janeiro and São Paulo. In short, the extensive model was characteristic of the traditionally populated areas of the Northeast and Southeast.

Concerning agricultural mechanization, in ESG TT1-27-57 Document, the professor goes on to point out that prior to its mechanization a technification of land works is necessary in order to that man can take full advantage of the machine and treats the educational perspective of the problem, requiring an enlightened farmer to choose the right machine for his services (p. 53).

In this logic, it is emphasizing that the problem of agriculture is not to do the work in less time, but to obtain a bigger production. In this way, the care with the correct use of the technique and the choice of the appropriate machine, would make the difference. In addition, it criticizes the lack of spare parts for the variety of sources of imported tractors in the agricultural modernization program.

It proposes an urgent plan for the financing of national agricultural machinery, to be supplied to farmers, which would guarantee the conservation of the machine and its spare parts. The intensification of the mechanization of agriculture, if it is possible to achieve greater soil mobilization, without the necessary protection against erosion, would contribute to the acceleration of soil erosion, especially in temporary crops. In addition, it emphasizes that the practice of burning, under unfavorable conditions, contributes to the impoverishment of the soil.

As for land ownership, when it speaks of the need for agricultural exploitation in real demographic voids, it says of the seriousness of the permanence, in reduced hands, of large tracts of land economically exploitable in the old ones and even in the new areas which are conducive to agricultural exploitation. More serious, he says, is the retention, without any kind of cultivation, of properties located on the periphery of urban centers, waiting for appreciation for speculation (p.66). He makes this distinction as important for the studies of the Brazilian Agrarian Reform. On agricultural credit, he concludes that every process of economic development requires a high investment contest (p.81).

Federation, according to data of the Ministry of Agriculture, in 51 pages of his work.

[71] BACHA,E.L. *Os mitos de uma década: ensaios de economia brasileira.* Rio de Janeiro, Paz e Terra, 1976, p.157.

[72] PATRICK,G. *Fontes de Crescimento na Agricultura Brasileira: o setor de culturas,* in C.R. Contador (org), Tecnologia e desenvolvimento agrícola. Rio de Janeiro, IPEA, 1975.

He sees agrarian credit as a much broader function than the simple conception
of credit as a substitute for exchange value, since it has the function of long-term
financing and many to the bottom. He criticizes "Banco do Brasil"'s (Bank of Brazil)
Agricultural Credit Portfolio, since it benefits the large farmer, due to the set of
demands and guarantees requested from the small farmer who cannot attend. The
conclusions that are possible to be organized from his work highlight the
appreciation of the Brazilian agriculture: 1) that the increase of the agricultural
production has been superior to the increase of the population of the country; 2) that
the increase in production, even if it corresponds to the increase in the area of
production, is also due to the increase in productivity, in an increasing index; 3) that
these facts do not indicate a better food index in the country, since there are
difficulties to establish the necessary uniformity of distribution; 4) that in the last ten
years agricultural production has been showing slower sensible growth, both in
subsistence production and in export production.

Exhorting the Ministry of Agriculture to reduce the negative aspects related to
land tenure for production relations with industry, encourages a rigid policy of
encouraging agricultural production. It is incumbent upon the Ministry of Agriculture
to promote, as a suggestion of it: a) economic development of production agriculture
throughout the country; b) economic stability of agriculture and livestock, through
specialized credit, guaranteed minimum prices, etc; and, c) a rational agrarian reform,
within democratic standards, not only facilitating access to land, but also establishing
real technical assistance resulting in broad technification.

The basis for the formulation of an agrarian policy commissioned by ESG would
follow the following approach (pp. 127-128): "Since it is not enough to give without
teaching how to use the elements of the factors of production, we believe that a real
policy will be based on the following points: 1) The access of the economically
sufficient worker, and especially the acquisition of the property, by the medium and
small farmer, should be valued by means of financing. The unproductive large farm and
the anti-economic small farm must be fought; 2) To value land and man through
technical assistance (the agricultural extension program[73]) in order to ensure that work
provides a decent existence for the farmer and the family; 3) Facilitate agricultural
credit that should be cheap, easy and personal; 4) Promote the training of large
numbers of technicians and take all possible measures to rid rural people of illiteracy; 5)
To intensively develop the agronomic research work, so that, using the results obtained,
one can achieve greater production per area.

To finish the technical series of documents, another work in the same line, a
simple lecture to the students of the Class of 1958 is what is about the
"Modernization of Agricultural Production". The lecturer, also professor, Álvaro
Barcelos Fagundes[74], establishes, as a rule, the specifics of the previous one,

---

[73] The agricultural extension, in its understanding is to technify agriculture, that is, the action of extending
to the farmers the studies and the effects of experimental research.

[74] Agronomist Engineer. Phd in the USA. He was director of the Institute of Economic Research of
Pernambuco, director of the Institute of Agricultural Experimentation, director of the National
Agricultural Research Service, agricultural attache to the Brazilian Embassy in Washington. At the time of
the lecture he was a member of the National Research Council and Advisor to the Development Council.
Your conference is an ESG document *C-61-58-Reservada.*

commenting on the particularities of agricultural production for laymen, the economic aspects of production and how to handle the problems of agricultural work in a very generic way. In his conclusions, he emphasizes that "the rapidly expanding food needs of the country's population and of materials for an important sector of the industries under intense development make the modernization of agriculture a national imperative" (p.24).

The noticeable but modest increase in the contribution of technological innovation to improved crop yields from the mid-1950s coincided with a general shift in the direction of agricultural development towards an active promotion of productivity growth.

Federal agricultural investments continued to be dominated by transportation and warehousing programs, as in the 1956-61 Plan of Goals.

However, in the early 1950s measures were introduced to accelerate technological innovation, which became increasingly important over the decade, foreshadowing the dominant role they would play in the agricultural policy of the following decade.

Given the priority to controlling urban food prices, these measures were on the supply side, subsidizing inputs, especially fertilizers and machinery, and mainly through the granting of preferential exchange rates, tariff exemptions and tax incentives.

In the early 1960s, these instruments lost part of their importance, after gradual unification of the exchange rate system and the introduction of national fertilizer and agricultural machinery manufacturing programs; and were supplanted by special rural credit programs in which the low, often highly negative, real interest rate became the main subsidy mechanism for current production and capital costs in agriculture.

It is at least curious to see how the approach of the specialist of this work of the ESG, when proposing sensible changes in so many sectors of the land infrastructure, was collaborator of actions so important to his time, that without a doubt it was the interest of the ESG, like advisory body for the Presidency of the Republic.

Observing from another prism more political than economic, the Brazilian *bourgeoisie* became an instrument of development, in the late 1950s, due to the increasing demands of capital and technology. The prosperity of the leaders was maintained, but there was a serious subordination to foreign investors, which meant a loss of power compared to before 1930.

The problem of nationalist development was a camouflage. If developmental action took place in this period with the nationalistic entourage in the way it was intended, the debate would cause difficulties for the policy of Juscelino Kubitschek, who would use ISEB services for his projects.

Now, the ISEB criticized the facade that JK fed. "Structural nationalism" had been a necessary feature of authoritarianism since the 1930s, because the breakdown of the international division of labor and internal capitalist could be conceived without making the overwhelming flow of international economic and political forces more difficult.

The dichotomy of nationalism & developmentalism still presented the problem of the Cold War that conditioned libertarian movements to the interests of subversion of order. Even worse, if Cuba was applying to be the eastern "aircraft carrier", on the doorstep of America Cuba, soon after the revolution, violently implements its agrarian reform, redistributing property and becoming envied by the Latin American countries that saw there the hope of better distribution of income, whether it considered land as a commodity or a multiplier of agricultural production possibilities, outside the patronage's pocket.

Thus, it is not without reason that Professor Emilio of TT1-27-57 timidly suggests a "rational agrarian reform", within the limits of permissible "democracy", to a military establishment that is clearly contrary to this policy, since ESG in this already had a counterpoint with ISEB.

The TT1 47-60, composed as the first work of the class of Benedito Pio da Silva, in a synthetic way, approaches a very interesting suggestion. It suggests an "agricultural and technological revolution" that only the army would be able to sustain, due to its obligation, to be compulsory and to be free, amid the wave of agricultural modernization. In this sense, the Army could contribute to increase the qualification of the rural man, summoning him to his ranks or advising on agricultural management techniques, which would foster better regional and national development.

About the participation of the Army in agroproductive activities is that curiosity looms. Throughout the 50's, some articles were published in the Military Club and in the National Defense Review, within the context of the already commented context of the rural exodus from the industrialization forced by state interventionism.

There was a question that the Army was not one of the factors that led to the emptying of the camp due to the compulsory military service that removed conscripts from rural areas and transported them to the barracks, which were usually located in the urban area or periphery.

In order to affirm the advantages of conscription for a population weakened in possibilities such as recruitment in the municipalities, there are utilitarian allegations in the military discourse[75]: 1) from the Army's point of view, the conscript could ascend to the rank or career positions, through his intelligence, dedication, physical condition, character; in short, a path that, if well defined, would allow the elimination of exclusionary obstacles in the traditional lack of opportunities of the interior; 2) career ascension, allowing the access of improvement of economic condition, in the gradual increase of the salaries, would better develop their future and their offspring; 3) the conscript would have the educational role served by the Army, since it would alphabetize it, due to functional needs; 4) the extension of this role would meet a need to sanitize the Brazilian population in general; changes in habits and attitudes towards hygiene and hygiene care, also contributing to the increase of the quality of life; 5) the "nationalism" that would be embedded in him, would consider him transformed from "individual to Brazilian"; 6) The exercise of a specific activity of the military force could represent qualifications that can be safely used in civilian life (driver, tractor driver, cook or typist, for example). In the outline of the proposal, in 1952, an article comments[76] on the relationship between the Army, the rural exodus and the "Tiro de Guerra"(TG) (the small military unit or subunit managed by a sergeant and sometimes still located in specific areas in Brazil to maintain army presence as representative and military reserve formation obligatory).

The TGs, almost extinct entities of the Army due to the maturation of Brazilian military doctrine, could be reactivated to meet the specific needs of the rural

---

[75] See Revista Defesa Nacional nr 437, de Dez 50, pp.70-79
[76] Revista Defesa Nacional nr 452, de Out 52, pp.129-132

population, preventing human force displaced from agricultural activity from the interior to the center. The problem lay in the very weak demographic condition that might not involve the creation of an army representation in the interior that would not be interested in the collapse of its command and logistics unit throughout the national territory, spread in thousands of cases.

In August 1953, Nestor Duarte, an economic analyst, appears in National Defense Magazine nr 470 (pp.77-81), which extracts an article from the Economic Digest of January 1953. The article begins by establishing the deep interdependence relationship between urban and rural.

Agrarian reform should reach the countryside through the extended benefit to municipalities. Speaking of which there was no exodus for the cities, but for the capitals, it showed that the projection of the urbanization would not necessarily mean the rural exodus, since the Brazilian population had a certain tendency to the fixity. In this way, the author shows that he is fully in favor of measures that mobilize agricultural development opportunities and understands that the Army can participate in this.

The Army General Staff finally stands on the issue and begins by defining the rural exodus[77]:

> (...) the rural exodus, motivated by military service, consists of the usual transfer to the cities of those summoned from rural areas who, when they are licensed from the ranks, no longer return to the places from which they came.

The Army was concerned with the collapse of its influence through the multiplication of TGs, in order not to recruit individuals from the interior who ended up in the urban "world", to be sure, for some of the advantages presented. In addition, he feared a new advance of a new "fifth column" (Luiz Carlos Prestes Column): a possible subversive channeling that from the inside would take advantage of the low defense nature of a non-operational subunit like the TG, which traditionally only formed the Army reserve, providing only basic information, characteristics of the infantry fighter, in its instructional program.

So, it starts to eliminate the conscription (obligatory military service) farmers, maintaining the moderate configuration of TG in the national territory until today[78]. However, another aspect reflects the Army's support for the country's agricultural production.

The rational use of extensive tracts of land distributed to the Army could be earmarked for large-scale production, at a time when Brazil needed to increase its share of agricultural surpluses, and this happened.

For a short period, the Army eventually participated in this project, collaborating with the lands distributed to it, organizational means and human resources. Tradition has led to subsistence agriculture within military areas or barracks - the farms - which endures in some military units of the present time.

---

[77] Revista Defesa Nacional nr 497, de Dez 55, pp.03-12

[78] The only book in the Army Library's catalog of publications dealing with this approach is The Army and the Rural Exodus, edited in 1959, but dated December 1956. It is the official expression, via the Army Staff, of the positioning of Military Institution for the case.

The coffee crisis and the 1956 Targets Plan had subsidized modern inputs, especially fertilizers and machines, and various subsidies to agriculture, especially rural credits. If several resources were transferred to the countryside, it was clear that increasing the prestige of the military institution in a reconstruction program would result in a greater national projection, in addition to the extension of its budget, since the Army would benefit agreements with other ministries in this strengthening[79] of agricultural development.

The studies on the agrarian structure, the socio-agrarian necessities and the contributions for the formulation of agrarian policies: 1962-1964

The "agrarian problem in the Northeast region, the peasant leagues and the role of the clergy" is one of the documents commissioned by ESG during this turbulent period of Brazilian agrarian history. Its author, the commander Mauro de Carvalho Aguiar, air force officer, makes his first class work cataloged as TT1-25-62-Reserved, this time from the perspective of the "psychosocial expression of the National Power". This concept of the ESG doctrine needs to be presented (1997, p.92):

(...) It is the predominantly psychological and social manifestation of the interactive group of men and the means that constitute the National Power, capable of favoring the full realization of the person and of his possibility to contribute to the improvement of society, with a view to achieving and preserve the National Objectives.

But there is also a necessary development that is the conceptualization of National Power (p.48):

(...) It is the capacity that has the interacting set of the men and the means that constitute the Nation, acting in the conformity of the national will, to reach and to maintain the National Objectives.

Having said that, it is characterized a change of direction of the previous works, of agricultural nature commissioned by the ESG. The official begins by explaining the historical reasons for a northeastern "export economy, based on latifundio, monoculture and slavery" (p.2).

He approaches lucidly when he explains that the set of economic activities in the Northeast-the export-slave trade on the one hand, which monopolized the best land on the coast, and the livestock and small farming on the other, with the semi-arid regions-presented contradictory characteristics for the region: fragility and resistance to long periods of depression.

Fragility, since the main economic activity was due to the external market, which followed its own fluctuation.

Resistance to long periods of difficulty, because the concentration of income was

---

[79] Revista Defesa Nacional nr 508, de Nov 56, pp.77-79

exclusive, leaving little room for the generation of internal monetary flows.

In addition to the ideas of the conservative dualism (the reasons for the delay explained in the actions differentiated by the interior or the coast) that it appropriates, it is still possible to identify Gilberto Freire's ideas in his work, to affirm that slavery was not the main factor behind the delay.

Citing Caio Prado Júnior, he tries to explain the delay also by the extremely low cultural level of the colony.

He makes a quick tour of the transition to wage labor in the Northeast, arriving to establish that the problem of the abolition of slave labor resembles that of the Agrarian Reform, regarding the redistribution of property.

The strength of the work would move from the property of the slaveholder to the individual, with repercussions on the organization of production, on the use of factors of production, on the use and distribution of income.

As for these "reflexes", the northeast would not have been favored by significant income redistribution, since the lands that could be used by agriculture were already fully occupied. The caatinga and the semi-arid region already had evident signs of demographic pressure, so that the freed slaves had difficulty moving to the subsistence sector. On the other hand, the poorly developed urban sector would not absorb this free but incapable population, given the demands of the new division of labor.

Such barriers would have fixed these free men in the sugar region with low wages or compensation equivalent to what they received as slaves. Already in the Center-South, where there was plenty of land, could the slave take refuge in the subsistence sector, at the same time that the expansion of coffee plantations would open space for higher wages: income was redistributed and the domestic market strengthened (p. 8).

He concludes in this first part, explaining that abolition for the Northeast constituted a measure of a political rather than an economic character. The economic structure continued the same, without generating internal monetary flow, with a high concentration of income and with capacity to withstand long periods of retraction; stagnant economy, but with capacity to resist structural changes due to absence of pressures.

Approaching according to Celso Furtado, explains the cycle of underdevelopment, which generates poverty and backwardness, which, in turn, brings greater underdevelopment, reporting the main structural failures.

In addition, he speaks of the poor administrative policy of the federal government and the lack of plasticity of the Northeastern economy, which, disregarding diversification, adopted a conformist policy with local conservatism, bringing the situation to "degrading" levels:

a) stagnation of the great crop export expansion led to a continued horizontal expansion of subsistence agriculture and, consequently, to the demographic saturation of drylands. This fact would have made the region more vulnerable to the droughts phenomenon;

b) droughts drain human capital from the area;

c) an Indus would increase the concentration of income;

d) the wrong investment policy of the federal government would be giving priority to industrialization and relegating education, health and agriculture to a lower plane;

e) there would be evasion of private resources of the Northeast, in search of greater profitability (pp.10-11).

More heavily criticizes the government when it speaks of its high investments failed in the region.

The failure of its objectives would be due to the lack of global vision of the problems of the Northeast and "the partial diversion of funds for electoral purposes and the illicit enrichment of many. Instead of a policy, the federal government has until recently had a plethora of policies through government agencies which do not solve the problems, generates a deep generalized feeling of frustration "(p.12).

While criticizing these federal bodies that demonstrate the inertia of the central administration in dealing with the problems of the Northeast, it mentions favorably the SUDENE (Superintendence of development of the Brazilian Northeast) superintendent, approaching his ideas about the fallibility of DNOCS (National Department of Drought Control in Northeast Brazil), when he diagnoses that the great problem of the Northeast was in the limitation of the availability of water, when SUDENE points out that the nature of the soil and the use of the soil must also be computed.

In fact, the dam and improvements that the DNOCS damming program preached was linked to the support of large estates which received most of the channeled water. In addition, the partial diversion of DNOCS funds fed the electoral program and the cyclical domain of local patronage[80].

As explained, Celso Furtado takes the conservative dualist thesis further by constructing a model for the economies and slave societies that have been generated by the dependence on distant consumer markets and subordinated to external impulses to themselves. In its logic, once the external demand is exhausted, a long period of indefinite stagnation begins, due to the impossibility of modifying these structures through their own internal dynamics, that is, inside out.

Only a favorable external environment can reactivate or transform them. Thus, he opposes the rigidity of archaic-traditional and authoritarian structures in his political model-the dynamism of modern, capitalist, and democratic or open structures[81]. In this explanation for underdevelopment, Furtado tends to see it as an "autonomous historical process" in the words of Teixeira da Silva (1981)[82], therefore, the process resulted from the penetration of modern capitalist enterprises into archaic structures, with their engine being the demand (in the coffee economy, external demand in the first stage of import substitution industrialization, preexisting demand for manufactures).

Like this, in its scheme, archaic structures could only be broken by induction: tax reforms by the modern, urban and industrial sector.

In this case, the Agrarian Reform proposal was the necessary condition for the solution of the problem of low-price food production for the domestic market and the expansion of consumption of industrial goods.

But the main problem for the application of his ideas rested on the ideological dilemma of the Cold War period. In mentioning the Agrarian Reform proposal, it could be confused with other dualist currents considered "Marxist", who believed that

---

[80] Observe the discussion in the work: Operação Nordeste, Celso Furtado

[81] FURTADO,Celso.*Formação Econômica do Brasil*, Rio de Janeiro, Fundo de Cultura, 1959.

[82] *Op.cit*, p.44.

overcoming underdevelopment would depend on the bourgeois-democratic revolution, on the mobilization of the "populist alliance" against "feudal remains" (Teixeira da Silva, 1981, p. 44) and this was also viewed with great caution by the anti-nationalist military wing.

When Air Force Commander Mauro talks about Agrarian Reform alert to the term's idiom, used as a form of dispute of prestige, of votes and of diffusion of communist cause "that collide with the concept of democracy". It then revisits the picture of the Brazilian agricultural condition, listing many of the structural difficulties already mentioned. After this reinforcement, he cries out in the following words: "there is, therefore, a clear need to reform the Brazilian agrarian structure, since it presents an unsatisfactory functioning from an economic and social point of view"(TT1-25-62-Reserved ESG Doc, p.14).

Soon after, he considers the benefit that the reform will bring to the man of the field and again he says: "it will necessarily succeed in correcting the distortions of the socio-economic panorama of the Brazilian countryside". Among these recommendations, it would be emphasized that Agrarian Reform is a human problem before being technical; Agrarian Reform can happen in the demo form not exclusively on the change in the status of rural property, but cannot dispense with its revision; the valorization of man can only happen through education; technicization and agricultural extension are necessary; the donation of land is not good practice: it must be sold, even long-term payment; large farms are conservative barriers to national development (p.18). The problem of education is, in its view, crucial for Agrarian Reform.

As part of his work, Jânio Quadros, at the request of SUDENE, would have appointed a Working Group chaired by Professor Ernesto Luiz de Oliveira Júnior to study the working conditions of universities and institutes of higher education in the Northeast and recommend measures to increase their efficiency in the development cooperation of the region.

Such a working group, in a masterful report, would have pointed out the low income of the universities of the Northeast. It suggests a quinquennial plan for the improvement of facilities and human resources, as a result of this group work, Jânio Quadros created by decree GRUNE (Technical-Scientific Re-equipment Group of the Northeast).

He accuses Goulart's "labor" government of freezing the plan and "confining himself to shaking the Grassroots Reforms and fighting tooth and nail by the plebiscite" (p.22), limiting Agrarian Reform without adequate assistance.

He speaks of a sabotage that would be made with the Alliance for Progress, since groups linked to the federal government (João Goulart) consider it as a scouring agent. The claim in paragraph 16 of the Art of the 1946 Constitution that cash compensation for expropriation is necessary for him is the argumentation of the conflict of main ideas.

The federal government, by failing to address the issue conscientiously and responsibly through the prior presentation of short- and long-term regional planning guidelines and programs, would have led public opinion and the landowners and their associations to elicit great opposition. Quote John Goulart in his unhappy sentence in Santos, May 13, 1962: "I am in favor of paying the owner, but that the value be paid at the level of what can be paid and that the payment be made in the long run and in any bonds of the Union, but not in money "criticizing him, for the buyer could pay what he pleased, characterizing a typical measure to refresh the moods in his government. Eugênio Gudin comments that also highlights the elasticity of the criterion.

It calls for confiscation of Goulart's actions and open confiscation of the "communists", criticizing both and proposing the intervention of the State in favor of the social performance of land ownership according to Art.147 of the Constitution of 1946, which empowers it of the soil and, in order to avoid social imbalances, to practice the intervention.

On the Peasant Leagues, it speaks of its origin, showing the mass of the Brazilian rural population living in the lowest social class, in a collapse and more absolute abandonment.

He says that "the Brazilian communist party soon turned its attention to the fertile terrain of the peasant mass, notably the northeastern peasant of the "Zona da Mata" agro-industrial region" (p.36).

In addition, according to information obtained by the National Security Council and the State Security Department of Pernambuco, it is from 1946 that the first rural associations known as peasant leagues are registered. In his ideology were the lessons of the Chinese revolution which advised the transfer of the "Party" center of activity to the rural districts, where the governmental police reaction was weaker and slower than in the cities, especially after the clandestinity of the PCB (Brazilian Communist Party) in 1947 (p.36).

The multiplication of these leagues would have led to the foundation, in 1950, of the Federation of Farmworkers and Peasants of the State of Pernambuco, "an umbrella body oriented to direct and direct peasant claims, to provoke misunderstandings between owners or residents and owners, sabotage in the sugarcane plantations and openly preach radical Agrarian Reform, that is, the violent appropriation of land by the peasantry."

He explains that, with Nikita Kruschev's policy diverging from that of Beijing, after Stalin's death, resulted in the split between the PCB. From the weakening of the PCB, weakened by the exodus of its intellectuals, the Agricultural and Livestock Society of the Planters of Pernambuco (p.38) was formed in 1955.

The growth of the activities of the leagues led to an interesting political projection of its leaders or supporters. Francisco Julião was elected state deputy and Miguel Arraes, mayor of Recife. With this, the initial headquarters of the "leagues" leaves from Vitória do Santo Antão to Recife, improving its representativeness.

The proliferation of the alloys is registered by the researcher, who also accompanies it in Paraíba and Goiânia. He cites a booklet of "communist indoctrination," the Cade of the Brazilian People, which is signed by Francisco Julião, Nelson Werneck Sodré and others.

He comments on excerpts from notebook number 1 which, according to him, gives a clear idea of the objectives, structure, operation, tactics of enticement of Peasant Leagues (pp. 40-47).

He says that Francisco Julião took advantage of the PCB crisis and organized himself via PC do B, trying to legitimize himself as an instrument of social upheaval in Brazil. It understands, however, the Peasant Leagues as a manifestation of the legitimate and democratic right to associate.

For him, the problem is to use regional deficiency to eliminate democracy. When commenting precisely on the origins of the peasant movement, its structure and techniques in Brazil, the official demonstrates a marked knowledge of the reality propitiated by the cold war in the midst of crises of power in the Eastern bloc, in an attempt to maintain the balance of world power.

China and Cuba had proclaimed a model of revolution distinct from the Soviet model, and revolutionary action in the case of underdeveloped countries seemed to be more efficient from the periphery to the center, valuing the places where the presupposition of social inequality so proposed.

The independent communist current that formed there, characterized by the splitting of the "partition", received wide support from Red China and Cuba; broad publicity and frequent possibilities abroad, in a frank proselytizing in competition with the US block, well represented by Latin America, but we must consider that Julião also received with open arms the American aid of the Alliance for the Progress.

The upsurge of the ambiguous presence of power in the Northeast has aroused American interest, which also comes from the struggle for oligarchic control and information from the follow-up of the trade union movement. In any case, "socialist" currents pursued similar goals, diverging only in the means to their reach.[83]

One can consider its internationalist influence, since it would also serve the expansionist interests of the Eastern bloc and in Brazil it seems to have acted in a complementary way: the official PCB would act, preferentially in the syndical sector of the urban workers and its dissidence, Luiz Flávio Carvalho Costa marks in "Rural Syndicalism in Construction", the beginning of modern Brazilian syndicalism in the mid-50's, even though he considers his work to be in the rural, student and in the various fields, with infiltration techniques at the beginning of the next decade.

Such an impulse has a severe participation after the 20th Congress of the CPSU, when there was a serious internal crisis of the PCB (1996, p. 46), allowing a faction and a different ideological vision.

In a collision course with the proposal of peaceful coexistence, the proposal of this Congress that would guide the new strategic base of Julião, with the Peasant Leagues, shows such diversity by organizing resistances from the Northeast and presenting a proposal to suppress the bourgeoisie while class, bringing the stage of the discussion not to the problem of Brazilian nationality threatened by US imperialism but to the difficult relationship between Capital and Labor, a proposal that threatened pro-USSR negotiations for an improvement of its image in Brazil, weak after the failure in 1935 and with the consequent entry into illegality (PCB was rehabilitated in 1945, militating in the field in the form of peasant leagues, soon to enter into lawlessness-1947).

In proposing a radical agrarian reform of the power structure, Julião wanted to assert that he underestimated the role of the PCB in the direction of the revolutionary movement (1996, p. 86). In his role, he brought severe criticism to the Communist Party's performance, gathering sympathy for his cause and enticing undecided categories of the same party.

It is in this environment that the Brazilian State, already worried about the possibility of the Catholic Church also reinforcing the left's control over the unionization of the field, fails to ignore the extension of the leftist party agenda and its

---

[83] See discussion in *A Operação Nordeste*, de Celso Furtado

political articulation. The threat posed by the unsustainability of the order in the field would represent serious damages to the electoral continuity and its conservative dominion in an environment as typical as the Northeast, which probably would have led, among other reasons, to the rupture of the conservative military in relation to Goulart, since he was in favor of grassroots reforms that made the balance for forces not completely conservative.

In the monograph, first class work, TT1 46-63-Reserved, the Agronomist Balbino Bastos France composes under the mission of "Analyze the National Environment in relation to Agriculture, Livestock and Fisheries. To suggest measures to increase the productivity of activities in those sectors, by raising the level of technology and rationalization.

Consider the needs of Development and Security. In this way, he analyzes the economic structure necessary for Agrarian Reform, opting it in function of the high index of concentration of ownership and control of the land; unproductive large farms; high proportion of rural workers among the rural population; preponderance of medium farms or small farms; low worker productivity; low levels and standards of living, and extreme degrees of social stratification.

He proposes that, as a general rule, all agrarian law should be supplemented by an agrarian plan, because if the former imposes regulatory principles, the latter concretizes and disciplines rural activity.

He also emphasizes that man must be the key to the process of agrarian development. In another work of the same sequence, TG1 14-63, Group Work led by Army Colonel Olavo Duarte Mendes, under the theme: "Agrarian Reform in Brazil"[84].

Despite the expectation that the theme provokes, due to this historical cut so characteristic, the document has a strong technical interpretation. But despite this, he reports that the great political problem for agrarian reform "is the result of the PTB (Labor Party) being in power" (p.18).

The PTB would have made commitments to the constitutional reform for the expropriation of land in advance payment in cash.

There was a fear from the UDN that, with the approval of the new constitutional text proposed by João Goulart's "Reforms", the PTB could do the expropriations, using this precious political instrument against the rural oligarchies largely supporters of the UDN and the PSD.

The work says that Brazilian agriculture did not keep up with the productivity progress observed in other countries of the world. The benefit of productivity, as you understand it, must meet three classes of beneficiaries: owners, workers and consumers.

Strictly speaking, this increase in productivity could be achieved without any new legislation, mobilizing entities for the development of actions and for the technical training of trainees. Amendments to legislation should have a favorable effect on the rural wage earner. Greater industrialization in the city would attract surplus labor in the countryside.

He says that it is necessary to consider the regional diversity of agrarian problems. The "cooperative" seems to be the only way of avoiding the consolidation of large

---

[84] The group consisted of two bachelors, two professors and four soldiers from the Army, Navy and Air Force, one of them a General.

properties, since, by strengthening cooperation among small ones, they could compete with large ones. Agrarian Reform should be a tangible reality of a global process of national economic development.

As for TG1 15-64, Group work led by Army Colonel Álvaro Cardoso[85], who is synthesized and who developed a theme imposed by ESG in order to appreciate the political, economic and social aspects of the Brazilian agrarian structure. According to the mission imposed on the group, it should indicate, "in the interest of National Security, a policy of reforming that structure aimed at the development of the country and correcting social injustices" (p.1).

It explains that a proposal of agrarian law must remove or reform the general conditions of life that suppress the common good. To this end, it proposes that the agrarian law should contain provisions that apply throughout the national territory, while the Rural Statutes should take greater account of regional peculiarities. It considers that the distribution of the property, in the Brazilian rural environment, represents a social injustice regarding the difficulties for the development and the improvement of the conditions of life of the Brazilian population that is dedicated to the field.

It blames the large rural properties that prove to be a powerful factor of delay, namely, the unproductive ones, which constitute an obstacle to economic progress and to the well-being of the populations.

Historically, it explains that the large farm was not created. It arose from the relations of production and was based between owner and worker, man and earth, fixing itself on the "trinomial-great property, slave-arm, inadequate technique" (p.3). The authors comment that the history of the land regime has been a struggle of two tendencies among the Brazilian people: the first, aristocratic rooted in the colonial land system that distorted the institution of the "sesmarias" (agrarian systems adopted by Portugal to colonize) and neutralized the attempt to combat the monopoly of land; and the other democratic, which, by possession and colonization, tries to break such device.

As for the Brazilian agricultural panorama that intends to study, establishes a composition of three types of agriculture for Brazil.

Regarding the first type, it comments on a fundamentally extractive feature operating in large regions of the country, notably for the production of rubber in the Amazon; chestnuts and wood; in Maranhão, for the production of "babaçu", operating in a large number of States with negative effects of devastation of the forests for the production of wood.

The second type, the most widespread, is what it calls "labor agriculture," characterized by excess labor and lack of technical equipment, which moves the cultures to new areas, leaving the primitives abandoned and almost barren for the lack of a rational application of fertilizers and processes of conservation of the ground. As for the third type, it mentions the "capital agriculture" that marks another structure at a much more advanced stage.

For the group, this would be the ideal for increasing the country's agricultural production. In logic, the work of man being replaced by the machine values the land for the good usufruct provided by it. As for the interest of National Security, it declares essential and urgent the realization of a reformulation of the relations between the

---

[85] The group consisted of four officers (one general) and five civilians, plus a liaison (a colonel).

structural elements - man, land and society - but this reform must be of an "evolutionary, never violent" tendency (p. 25).

If these considerations were not met, national interests would be increasingly compromised, since the valorization of man and greater agricultural productivity were part of the "National Power "In their respective fields of influence. On Agrarian Reform, he points out that only emphasizing it by the bias of the land and its economic purpose, despising the "man", escapes the high social objectives necessary. This time, it proposes that the agrarian law should have a national ambience, respecting the regional peculiarities by means of rural statutes addressed to it.

Oscar de Hollanda Moreira's end-of-course monograph, TT4 08-68, is governed by the theme: "Relate and analyze the fundamentals and factors of the Economic Field, in order to allow the production of information for a strategic assessment of the agricultural sector, characterizing the possibilities and vulnerabilities of the current land reform policy. This research should provide data for an estimate of the next five (05) years".

He summarizes that the Superintendency of Agrarian Reform (SUPRA), serving the dominant interests, was extinguished with the regime of 1964 and that the Castelo Branco government began to take serious care of the agrarian question, not only in its social aspect as in the economic one.

TT1 38-69, a Gutemberg end-of-course monograph from Costa Brito, is summarized in the perspective of surveying the main obstacles to the agrarian reform program, calling for urgent technical measures. It elaborates a proposal for the development of the Northeast, discriminating laws and procedures. He declares that the existing reforms have been more social than economic.

The document suggests the creation of cooperatives or small-farm incentives. The interesting preparatory approach that the Land Statute and the implementation of the Agrarian Reform-conference given by Paulo de Assis Ribeiro, president of the Brazilian Institute of Agrarian Reform (IBRA), makes directing the work for the Statute of the Terra, leads us to understand the development of the process of a new political-land establishment, after the establishment of the regime of force of 1964.

He says that after 1964, a Working Group was constituted by the Government to prepare documents that should serve as a basis for the drafts of the constitutional amendment and the Land Statute, having been submitted to the consideration of political parties, the Confederation and the Rural Federations, the Confederation of Rural Workers, the Secretaries of Agriculture of the States and the various specialized entities, before being sent to the National Congress by the President of the Republic.

He considered two key concepts that were basic to the agrarian action of the government: 1) Agricultural Policy defined as "promotion of measures of protection of rural property that are intended to guide, in the interests of the economy of the primary sector, agricultural activities, to guarantee them full employment, or to harmonize them with the process of industrialization of the country; 2) Agrarian Reform defined as" the best distribution of land and the establishment of a system of relations between man, rural property and land use, so that the principles of Social Justice and increased productivity are respected and respected, to guarantee the progress and well-being of the rural worker, as well as the development of the Country, with a gradual and progressive extinction of the large farm". (p.5)

The categorization of the ideas expressed by ESG in the search for solutions to the agrarian problem

As pointed out in the brochure dealing with the "Doctrinal Foundations of the ESG" (1997, p. 83), the so-called "changes in socio-economic behavior" are categorized within the objectives of recomposition of the economy by the spatial expansion of the market, power centers by the formation of megablocks and to enable the existence of new and different patterns of production.

The reorganization of the monocultural system, which could aid in the problem of the supply of agricultural products, is now well known to ESG students. The technicization of agriculture as an instrument for the improvement of capitalist production relations is in the order of the day of studies.

The amount of exports of agricultural products influencing the capacity of the Brazilian trade balance, besides contributing to the potential of domestic consumption, would avoid the evasion of foreign currency by the weakened land structure and full of archaisms.

The influence of CEPAL's ideas (Commission for the Development of Latin America) in some of the works is observable and this demonstrates the credibility of the conception that the theoretical and practical changes that were proposed to know and apply, when necessary, would imply in reforms as deep as the condition of fragility of the failure of the system monocultural classic.

If we mention the lack of an agricultural framework for the expansion of market capacity, this is associated with industrial security, in the sense of the stability of the economy based on industrialization and that indirectly would suffer the side effects of the lack of technicization for the management of agriculture and the transformation of the raw material of the field into consumer goods, whether internal or external. This emphasis on technicization, as recorded in the documents of the School, would lead to an optimized use of labor, qualified and well endowed with technological instrumentation.

In this way, there seems to be a military culture that privileges the instrumentalization of the man of the field, but in such a culture the vision of the development of the individual as a whole is not detected. The social that is proclaimed before the logic that the School adopts of developing a country of social welfare (Welfare State), is far from distancing itself from the rhetoric.

The general discourse is of the production of material and salutary benefits to the growth of the corporate body, in a demonstration of the continuous predilection for the structuralism of the ESG's work, but that is not corresponding with the care of the harmonious growth of the agrarian society in its conflicts and contradictions.

This methodology, fragmentary in nature, but didactically effective for the projection of scenarios, privileges the agrarian macrocosm (a privilege that is accentuated by the preservation of the conservative power game in the peasantry), to the detriment of the corresponding microcosm.

At the root of the problem to be worked out, in the rigor of the method applied in the ESG, there is the isolation of the class question that also encompasses the reality of the Brazilian peasantry. As an obstacle to the uprising, are the oligarchies that constitute a serious advance to the technicization. This, in turn, stimulating the collectivization, the cooperativism or the progress of the small and medium-sized agro-industrial company highlights a great contrariety of the proposal.

As for the mass use of agricultural implements, once again the interest is observed to exclude from the daily life of the farmer the old management techniques that would not be effective to increase the individual productive capacity of the field. The diffusion of management techniques, especially emphasis on soil care, which receives the attention of fertilizers and correctives, is also linked to the industrialism of the period. In this movement of increasing the productivity of the soil, through application of correctives, there is mention of an incentive for the development of the industry of fertilizers and correctives.

Consequently, as a consequence, the improvement of the regional transport network is sought to reduce costs with the disposal of this production. The low storage capacity of the sector is also mentioned in appropriate silos and warehouses, which, together with the mentioned factors, no longer favors the improvement of the agricultural productivity result.

If the illiteracy of the individual of the field enters as a component of the process of diminishing results, at no moment does the concentration of the specific interest on the citizen, but on the instrumentalized agent of progress, accompanied solely as a form of performance.

It is observed in the selected works an interest in the junction of agriculture with the industrialization project. This is consistent with the limits of structural development imposed by the incentives received since 1930 with the strengthening of American capitalism in Brazil.

New forms of intervention in industry, technical cooperation with the US, including military aid provided by the US-Brazil Military Agreement, allowed for a diversification of economic and financial performance. The ex an objective of the "Economic Expression of National Power", in this sense, would lead to this popular support of a political and social nature for the change of the land structure.

Even if it were known that the re-equipping of the Brazilian park by the American resources would result in a rearticulation of classes and socio-economic groups in the effort to denationalize the process, the resistance to change was enormously greater, to the point of diminishing the power of the reforms. From this point of view, national security was affected, in view of the documents, since progressivism required the reduction of the border between the rural and the urban.

When the conservative dualist conception enters stage studies, the immobility of the interior becomes seen as a pathological reason for affectation to the social organism by the ESG doctrine and is well-suited. If man were to overcome the resistance of the archaic, accepting the entrance of capital, technique and progress, the modification of the land structure would not be necessary, since localism would be able to produce without the erosion of conflicting political forces by the dispute of oligarchic power, traditionally resistant to correctives in the North and Northeast regions of the country.

The knowledge of the geophysiological conditions of the interior areas and the lack of education of the rural workers seems to be treated seriously in the governmental plans, would correspond to the estimated productive proficiency, from the interior. But we must consider that these ideas of reformulation of the structure circulate through the works seen.

When Celso Furtado deepens the solutions to remove the delay of the field, his ideas are used and reproduced in some of the selected works. The inclusion of the marginal population in capitalist relations of production through conflict with the regional patronage, however, provoked strange reactions within the conservative military elite that feared the social imbalance in the Northeast.

The political-ideological manipulation of the problem was his greatest fear, for without the appropriate partisan support in these areas of strong exclusion from opportunity, there was all the room for subversion and consequent imbalance of the conservative power of the Armed Forces in the national territory, in the projection of its influence.

That is why the proposal of an agrarian reform appears within democratic standards, where the alignment with the US would not be harmed. The relation between agricultural production and national industry should be restricted to the elements, to the factors of production, specifically.

There was no interest and it is not found in the material observed, to escape the rigor of agricultural technification that facilitated the commercial and political relationship with the US and that modified four century of relationship of dependence with the European metropolis in the agrarian-mercantilist export. It is suggested understood as a point of support for an agricultural and technological revolution in this wave of agricultural modernization.

Once again, increasing the qualification of the man who passes through their ranks or through technical advice to the peasant, is the progressive logic that imbues itself in the developmentalist project. National-developmentalism, lacking in profound reforms is severely countered by the reasons already raised, but the pendent role of ISEB-ESG appears in the discussion of the theme.

Some of the reformist ideas of the ISEB are absorbed, even in a respectful way, in some of ESG's works. To say that agrarian reform is a human problem before being a technician does not characterize ESG's thinking, although it seems that it is. From the second half of the 1950s we see an approach of technicization coupled with a caution with the evolution of social disloyalism proclaimed in the reformist or revolutionary proposal, contrary to liberal ethics.

At the end of the government of Juscelino Kubitschek, the Institute for Research and Social Studies (IPES) and the Brazilian Institute for Democratic Action (IBAD) were sown in politics. Its connection with the military-techno-bureaucratic mechanism was narrow and far surpassed the study and the actions for the political mobilization in the field.

However, the brown eminence of these institutes against the government of João Goulart, who had exploited the reforms as the vocation of his planning, gave the liberal counterweight, protecting the Brazilian business and industrialist program in which the ESG military were included. The IPES was presented to society as an entity also of a populist nature, aiming at the cultural, moral and civic education of individuals and showing concern to develop studies and activities of a social nature. It acted as the front entity of the aforementioned mechanism, mobilized for the deconstruction of the opposition to the liberal project.

The covert side coordinated a sophisticated and multifaceted military political and ideological campaign (Dreifuss, 1981, p.164). The founders of IPES were dedicated to work as a strategic unit, supported by the IBAD as a tactical unit. When there is mention of the peasant leagues, an understanding of the strengthening of trade unionism in the countryside appears and how this may be threatening to the liberal influence supported by this military antinationalist segment, but this threat is clothed in the cold war environment.

The Northeast, as an area of confrontation of party politics, is being characterized as the main focus of misalignment of the industrialization program, due to its differences and inequalities.

But the structural reforms that are called for have not been answered in a liberal way, nor could they be, since the depth of the problem: the transformation of the logic of usufruct to that of sanitation of the area by the human way not coupled with the traditional relations of production was being used as a populist and ideological propaganda of the opposite segment to the bureaucratic-business interest, with the support of the Armed Forces majority, at that moment, and in this vision of American alignment.

Even when one observes the documents closest to the Statute of the Earth in 1964, it is seen that the Agrarian Reform is still approached in a strictly technical way, stripping away the character, necessarily, ideological. Thus, when the resistance of the opposition in the regime of force of 64 has expired, the new measures for the conciliation of moods in the problem of the Northeast are announced, mainly.

The extinction of large farm, the protection of small rural property for harmonization with the country's industrialization, as well as a system to facilitate the relationship between man, rural property and land use are proposed by the Brazilian Institute of Agrarian Reform (IBRA), although it is already a well-known discourse in the revision of the production of the ESG in the decades of 50 and 60, that now is of much greater importance, so that urgent measures, which have been postponed, can be implemented in full military government avoiding compromising their credibility.

5 CONCLUSION

In these considerations it is intended to return to some of the conclusions already present in the course of each chapter, as final reflections.

At the beginning of the work, the problem of the description of ESG thinking lies within the question of what the School is actually.

Considered as an opinion-maker by the civil world, and thus responsible for almost all the great Brazilian political maneuvers of more than forty years of intense world dichotomy, curiosity becomes appropriate.

The dissection of the ESG eschews the specificity of this work, but the military thinking and its nuances was not evident in it, even in its contradictions. But why study the military apparatus in a reading so delineated, if the enriching focus of this work focuses on reading the military vision before the Agrarian Question?

The answer lies in the difficulty in understanding the phenomenon without understanding how the military segment is organized, even in a fractional way.

Military chains, although they may appear as military parties, do not fail to maintain an order, a legality considered minimum for the military honor and the preservation of ethics, in the end the military axiological complex that must be studied in a special way.

In this regard, it is sufficient to review what has been commented on the assumption that Brazilian officials have been formed in the forcible belief in their vocation as elite, for the government, to the detriment of the lack of seriousness of the Brazilian institutions and men.

If this seems an affront and demeanor to the keen observer, what to say when it becomes a reality in the ESG Project?

Therefore, this may be the reason for this depth at the beginning of the work. In addition, the conservative thinking of the Military Institution is remarkable in the methodology of ESG studies. If authoritarianism in these moments of veiled democracy is also veiled speech, how understand the truth of its purposes?

The influence of authoritarian thought in all works is astonishing, and it must also be traced back to the Catholic ethic that precedes us.

In any case, in accompanying the study of the doctrine of the School and its political-pedagogical process, we think intensely of Gramsci's view of the co-optation of the elites and of their organization of the process of domination of power, from the superior structures of power.

ESG is as perfectly fitted in design as in oppression, if necessary. This characterized itself and stigmatized it.

If many of the truths can be revealed now, when the content protection of some of its documents is out of date and made available for this work, one can notice the seriousness of serious researchers who preceded us in works of high level of difficulty and excellence. This is also visible here.

Throughout the second chapter, attempts are made to establish the contradictions of this military thinking in confrontation with literature and before the testimony of active and illustrious responsible for the process of grounding the role of the School within Brazilian society, but also is very concerned about the division of the military in the search for the power of the institution.

The classic discussion between positivists and professionalists is permeated by the "things of politics," when the anti-nationalist wing and the military nationalist struggle, marked by the case study of the Military Club. Again, it arouses the curiosity of military behavior for scholars, since the military nationalist wing does not have the same connotation of the nationalist movement so exploited by the Brazilian left in the 1950s and 1960s.

The rejection by socialism and its consequences within the Armed Forces would have reached a large number of adherents and military doctrine thus consolidated, considering spurious all other ideological alternatives for the military.

The fourth chapter deals with the contextualized Agrarian Question. One cannot see this work as an important element to understand it, but rather a military view of the problem.

A case study of the ESG with the use of exclusively available material that clarifies, from the point of view of the students, how the needs of the Presidency of the Republic can be met in relation to the National Security interests and the agricultural potential.

It is a question of identifying potential and not necessarily an exhaustion of the sources on the thought of the official ESG, until the access to the sources that would explicitly explain the still reserved documents of the School - the thought, were not consulted. Therefore, this space is formally open to be devastated.

This short essay attempts to point out the tendency that a researcher should have in his quest when examining these documentary sources of ESG. The cataloging of the subject-Agrarian Question-does not exists for ESG.

What exists is under the themes of Agriculture, Agriculture, Fisheries, Agricultural Policy, Agrarian conjuncture, Agrarian Reform; but they also suggest crossing with other subjects such as: politics and Brazil, economic field and agriculture, and so on.

From what has been raised, it is possible to identify a tenuous trend of a gradient in the approach to Agrarian Question.

Since the foundation of the School, it has been observed the dating of the documents that deal with the subject.

The survey of the agricultural potential and the proposed corrections that are requested to the students are accompanied by an effort on the part of the teachers to inform well and to lead the student body in the orientation of the work.

It is not simply an extension of general knowledge. This is a subsidy applied to student research, from the beginning of the school activity. Distinguished speakers are summoned to the platform and the theme is thus given the importance it really has.

The problem is that the task of instruction is not confused with that of teaching, but of forming, informing. Thus, there is an ellipse in the global view of agriculture in its theoretical-political-economic aspect.

As a rule, when the agrarian question is taken care of as the "economic expression of the National Power," one notices its interpenetration in other domains of power.

As to the tenuous gradient detected, the work is categorized in the periods 1949-1955, 1955 -1960,1962-1964 and from 1964 onwards, a little by 1964 to observe what happens in the full exercise of the government of force. In the period 1949-1955 a great effort is made for the expansion of the market capacity, with the emphasis given to the technification and the extension of agriculture to the peasants.

There is not much concern about the agrarian reform, even from the political point of view.

There is talk of agricultural development with mechanization, a proposal of agricultural modernization to increase internal and external trade: all in partnership with industrialism, in a remarkable way.

Man, as a factor of production, at this moment is seen only as instrumental agent of progress. One does not observe the care of educating it, noting it as an individual marginalized by the process of monocultural exclusion, but of instructing it in the use of modern forms of exploitation of the soil. T

he technification is thus hand in hand with the injection of foreign capital into Brazilian projects and hence the emphasis of the work commissioned from the students.

From 1955 to 1960 the study goes through a transition. Concerns with the land structure already exist and some CEPAL ideas materialize what is available of information to be consulted by ESG. SUDENE has a progressive force that is used and sometimes strengthens students' criticism of the phenomenon of concentration of land and power.

But this cannot be seen so logically. This phase also covers the study for the implementation of a complementary industrial park from the field. The moment is that of dualistic theses and the theoretical consideration of the delay of the field in relation to the urban seems to predominate.

The channeling of resources for agriculture, the efforts of the National Institutions to reduce the market gap that affects Brazilian productivity is undoubtedly the main point.

The Army, when it is called to participate in agricultural production effectively with instruction, men and equipment, denotes its priestly activity more than participatory.

A great effort was made to develop agricultural technicist and this can be seen in the documents.

From 1962-1964 the perspective of Agrarian Reform enters the picture, as it could not fail to be, due to the threats of the intensification of the political-ideological propaganda in Brazil and in particular by the displacement of part of the urban power axis towards the interior.

The peasant leagues show that the peasant citizen, who was not treated as such, should be more politically exploited in their differences. The corrective discourse appears in the documents of the ESG, which struggles to assert a welfare state, leading to the harmonization of the public and the private for the great national reconstruction project, from the focus on industry.

The man from the North and Northeast fields, "escoria" traditionally marked by the marginalization provoked by the relation of capitalist production, is seen as an element to be conquered, before the enticement of the left to do. As of 1964, the observed documents point to the pact of the military government with the categories in conflict.

The documents still point to technical reforms, but this time, for the elaboration of the Land Statute, we hear those who were in the dispute for agrarian power. Losers and winners are used to establish legislation to reduce the clamor of some centuries. The military government could not fail in the enterprise and the originality of the opportunity, after João Goulart failed in the attempt.

The ideas for a reform proposal that is more technical than ideological is the one that can be verified. Deep structural reforms are not implemented, but should be thought through and done under the program's articulation.

The logic was Brazilian branch of industry strengthening the economic groups and their influence in the field, to use it in the logic of commercial expansion. Thus, the delay in agricultural development is justified by the liberal mechanism of expansion and by the lack of interest in deepening the conflict with conservative forces-patronage and localism.

The expressive orientation of political action towards indiscriminate industrialization, in the tonic of "order and progress", went far beyond the true needs of the Brazilian peasantry, mystified and bestialized by ineptitude and commitment to the private to the detriment of the public, even among those who they claim to be champions of justice.

BIBLIOGRAPHY

BIBLIOGRAPHY AND SOURCES
Documentary Supplies and Archives
Arquivo Histórico do Exército-Palácio Duque de Caxias-Rio de Janeiro
Clube Militar-Rio de Janeiro
Biblioteca do Exército-Palácio Duque de Caxias-Rio de Janeiro
Escola Superior de Guerra-Rio de Janeiro

Journals
A Defesa Nacional. Rio de Janeiro.
Revista do Clube Militar. Rio de Janeiro.
Revista da Escola Superior de Guerra. Rio de Janeiro.

Newspapers
Folha de São Paulo. São Paulo.
O Estado de São Paulo. São Paulo.
O Globo. Rio de Janeiro.
O Jornal do Brasil. Rio de Janeiro.

Documentation
AGUIAR, Mauro de Carvalho.1962.*O problema Agrário na região Nordeste, as ligas camponesas e o papel do clero.* Rio de Janeiro, ESG-Doc. TT1 25-62.
ALENCAR, Fernando Ramos de.1956. *Conjuntura Nacional: Fatores Econômicos.* Rio de Janeiro, ESG-Doc. TG1 13-56.
ARAÚJO, José Emílio Gonçalves.1957.*Levantamento do potencial nacional efetivo.* Rio de Janeiro, ESG-Doc. TT1 27-57.
ARRUDA, Antonio de .1983. *A ESG: a história de sua doutrina.* São Paulo, Edições GRD.
BRITO, Gutemberg da Costa. 1969. *Análise da política de reforma agrária.* Rio de Janeiro, ESG-Doc. TT1 38-69.
CARDOSO, Álvaro.1964. *Estrutura Agrária Brasileira.* Rio de Janeiro, ESG-Doc. TG1 15-64.

CASTELLO BRANCO, Humberto de Alencar. 1964. *Discursos: 1964*. Brasília: Secretaria de Imprensa.

FAGUNDES, Álvaro Barcelos. 1949. Aspectos da Agricultura Brasileira.Rio de Janeiro, ESG-Doc A 014-49.

______1950. *Produção Agrícola*. Rio de Janeiro,ESG-Doc A 02-50.

______1958. *Modernização da Produção agrícola*. Rio de Janeiro, ESG-Doc C1 61-58

FARIAS, Osvaldo Cordeiro de. 1981. Meio século de combate: diálogo com Cordeiro de Farias, Aspásia Camargo, Walder de Góes. Rio de Janeiro, Nova Fornteira.

FILHO, Antonio José Rodrigues. 1969. *Aspectos para o Desenvolvimento da Agricultura*. Rio de Janeiro, ESG-Doc C 97-69.

FRANÇA, Balbino Bastos.1963. *Analisar a conjuntura Nacional em relação à agricultura, pecuária e pesca*. Rio de Janeiro, ESG-Doc. TT1 46-63.

GOÉS MONTEIRO, Pedro Aurélio de. 1934. A Revolução de 30 e a finalidade política do Exército. Rio de Janeiro, Adersen Editores.

GUERRA, Escola Superior de. 1993. *Manual Básico*. Rio de Janeiro.

______.1980. *Fundamentos doutrinários da Escola Superior de Guerra*. Rio de Janeiro.

______.1997. *Fundamentos doutrinários da Escola Superior de Guerra*. Rio de Janeiro.

GURGEL, José Alfredo de Amaral. 1975. Segurança e Democracia: uma reflexâo sobre a doutrina da Escola Superior de Guerra. Rio de Janeiro, José Olympio.

LEITE, Edgard Teixeira. 1963. *A Reforma Agrária*. Rio de Janeiro,ESG-Doc C 43-63.

LEMOS, Hygino de Barros. 1959. *O Exército e o Êxodo Rural*. Rio de Janeiro. Biblioteca do Exército.

LIMA, Rubens Rodrigues. 1964. *A agricultura no Brasil*. Rio de Janeiro, ESG-Doc. TT1 51-64

LIMA, Valentiva Rocha (Coord.) 1986. *Getúlio: uma história oral*. Rio de Janeiro, Record

LYRA TAVARES, Aurélio de. 1976. *O Brasil de minha geração*. Rio de Janeiro, Blblioteca do Exército.

MEINBERG, Iris. 1963. *Aspectos Particulares da Conjuntura Nacional: Panorama da agricultura e pecuária*. Rio de Janeiro, ESG-Doc C 26-63.

MENDES, Olavo Duarte. 1963. *A Reforma Agrária no Brasil*. Rio de janeiro, ESG-Doc.TG1 14-63.

MOREIRA, Oscar de Hollanda. 1968. *Informações para avaliação estratégica da Reforma agrária*. Rio de Janeiro, ESG-Doc. TT4 08-68.

MOTTA, Jehovah .1998. Formação do Oficial do Exército: currículos e regimes na Academia Militar, 1810-1944., Rio de Janeiro, Biblioteca do Exército

OLIVEIRA, João Cleofas de.1952. *Política Agrária Nacional*. Rio de Janeiro, ESG-Doc A 12-52

PEREGRINO, Umberto. 1966. O pensamento da Escola Superior de Guerra. Cadernos Brasileiros. Rio de Janeiro., v.8, n.38, Nov-Dez.

PEREIRA, Ivo Arzua. 1969. *Agricultura: Base e Garantia de Desenvolvimento e da Segurança*. Rio de Janeiro, ESG-Doc C 69- 69.

RIBEIRO, Paulo de Assis. 1965. *O Estatuto da Terra e a execução da Reforma Agrária*. Rio de Janeiro, ESG-Doc C1 85.

SARDENBERG, Idálio. 1987. Princípios Fundamentais da Escola Superior de Guerra. Rio de Janeiro. Revista da Escola Superior de Guerra. v.3, n.8.

SILVA, Benedito Pio da. 1960. *Estudos sobre a estrutura fundiária*. Rio de Janeiro, ESG-

Doc TT1 47-60.

SODRÉ, N.W. 1968. *História Militar do Brasil*. Rio de Janeiro. Civilização Brasileira

SOUZA, João Kessler Coelho de.1955. *A agricultura e Matérias Primas vegetais*. Rio de Janeiro,ESG-Doc.T1 29-55.

TÁVORA, Juarez.1948. O problema Brasileiro do Petróleo. Ensaio de Solução Objetiva, Rio de Janeiro.

______.1974. *Uma vida e muitas lutas*. Rio de Janeiro, José Olympio, 3v.

WALTERS, Vernon. 1986. *Missões Silenciosas*. Rio de Janeiro. Biblioteca do Exército.

References

ADERALDO, Vanda.1978. *A Escola Superior de Guerra: um estudo de currículos e programas*, mimeo, IUPERJ, Rio de Janeiro,

ALMINO, João. *Os Democratas autoritários*. São Paulo: Brasiliense, 1980.

ANDRADE JÚNIOR, H. Matrizes ideológicas presentes no segmento militar brasileiro: O Caso do Clube Militar. Comunicação Livre. In: *Encontro Regional De História, 21-25 Agosto,* 2000, Universidade Federal Fluminense. Campus do Gragoatá, Niterói: UFF.

BACHA, E.L. *Os mitos de uma década: ensaios de economia brasileira*. Rio de Janeiro, Paz e Terra, 1976.

BARROS, Alexandre. 1979. *Formando Elites*. Jornal da Tarde, 25 Ago79

BASTIDE, Roger. *Brasil, Terra de Contrastes*. São Paulo, Difusão Européia do Livro, 1973.

BELOCH, Israel & ABREU, Alzira Alves de. *Dicionário histórico —biográfico brasileiro (1930/1983)* . Rio de Janeiro: Forense-Universitária/ CPDOC/Finep,1984. 4 volumes.

BENEVIDES, Maria Victoria de Mesquita. *A UDN e o Udenismo* .Rio de Janeiro: Paz e Terra,1981.

______. *O governo Kubitscheck : desenvolvimento econômico e a estabilidade política*. Rio de Janeiro: Paz e Terra,1979.

BIELSCHOWSKI, Ricardo. *Pensamento Econômico Brasileiro (1930-1964)* 3 Edição. Rio de Janeiro: Contraponto,1996

BRIGAGÃO, Clovis.1978. *Brazil's Foreign Policy: The Last 15 years* . Mimeo, Institute of Latin American Studies, Stockholm.

BURGUESS, Mike & Wolf, Daniel. 1980 . *Brasil: o conceito de Poder na Escola Superior de Guerra*, in Revista de Cultura Vozes, ano 75, vol.LXXIV, n 5, jun/jul. Rio de Janeiro.

CAMARGO, Sonia. (s/d). *Militares e Geopolítica no Brasil*, mimeo, PUC- Rio de Janeiro.

CARVALHO, João Carlos M.de Carvalho. *Camponeses no Brasil*. Petrópolis:Vozes,1979

CARVALHO, José Murilo de.1982. *Forças Armadas e Política, 1930-1945*. In: A Revolução de 30. Seminário Internacional. Brasília: UNB editora, 1982..

______. *A Construção da Ordem*. 2 Edição. Rio de Janeiro:UFRJ/Relume-Dumará,1996.

CASTRO, Celso.1995. *Os Militares e a República: um estudo sobre cultura e ação política*. Jorge Zahar Editora, Rio de Janeiro, pp.63-64.

COELHO, Edmundo Campos. *Em Busca de identidade: o Exército e a Política na Sociedade Brasileira*. Rio de Janeiro: Forense Universitária,1978.

CORBISIER, Roland. *Reforma ou Revolução*. Rio de Janeiro: Civilização Brasileira,1968.

COSTA, Luiz Flávio C.*Sindicalismo Rural em construção*. Rio de Janeiro: Forense Universitária,1996.

DEBERT, Guita Debert. *Ideologia e Populismo*. São Paulo: TAC, 1979.

DINIZ, Eli . 1991. O *Estado Novo: estrutura de poder e relações de classe*, em HGCB, vol.III-Sociedade e Política (1930-1964), Bertrand Brasil Editora S.A, Rio de Janeiro.

DRAIBE, Sônia. *Rumos e metamorfoses: Estado e industrialização no Brasil (1930 –1960)*. Rio de Janeiro: Paz e Terra , 1985.

DREIFUSS ,René Armand. *1964 : A Conquista do Estado*. Petrópolis:Vozes,1981.

DULLES, John W.F. Dulles. *President Castello Branco, the Brazilian Reformer.* Texas: A&M University Press,1980.

FALCON, Francisco. *História e Poder* . In: CARDOSO, C.F.& VAINFAS, Ronaldo(orgs). Domínios da História: ensaios de teoria e metodologia. Rio de Janeiro: Campus,1997.

FAORO, Raymundo. *Os Donos do Poder.*11 Edição. São Paulo:Globo,1995

FARIAS, José & LAMOUNIER, Bolívar. 1981. *O futuro da abertura: um debate.* Cortez & IDESP Editoras, São Paulo.

FIGUEIREDO, Eurico de Lima. *Os militares e a Democracia.* Rio de Janeiro: Graal,1980.

FONSECA, Pedro Cesar Dutra. *Vargas : O capitalismo em construção.* São Paulo: Brasiliense,1989 .

FUCHTNER, Hans. *Os sindicatos brasileiros : organização e função política .* Rio de Janeiro: Graal, 1980.

FURTADO, Celso. *Um projeto para o Brasil.* 2 Edição. Rio de Janeiro: Saga,1968.

FURTADO,Celso. *Formação Econômica do Brasil,* Rio de Janeiro, Fundo de Cultura, 1959

GAIO, André Moysés. 1997. *Em Busca da Remissão: a Mobilização Militar pela Democracia.* UEL Editora, Londrina.

GOMES, Angela Maria de Castro (org).*O Brasil de JK.* Rio de Janeiro: Fundação Getúlio Vargas, 1991.

GRAMSCI, Antonio. *La Política y el Estado Moderno.* Barcelona: Planeta-De Agostini,1993

HIRST, Mônica. *A política externa do segundo governo Vargas.* Rio de Janeiro: Cpdoc, 1992.

IANNI, Octavio. *Ditadura e Agricultura.* Rio de Janeiro: Civilização Brasileira,1979

JAGUARIBE, Hélio. 1969. *Desenvolvimento Econômico e Desenvolvimento Político.* Paz e Terra, Rio de Janeiro.

LAMBERT, Jacques, *Os Dois Brasis.* Rio de Janeiro, INEP, Centro Brasileiro de Pesquisas Educacionais, 1959.

LAVAREDA, José Antônio.*A democracia nas urnas : o processo partidário eleitoral brasileiro.* Rio de Janeiro, IUPERJ,1991.

LEAL, Victor Nunes. *Coronelismo, Enxada e Voto.*3 Edição. Rio de Janeiro: Nova Fronteira,1997

LIMA, Valentina da Rocha (org) et alli (1986). *Getúlio, uma história oral.* Guavira Editora, Rio de Janeiro.

LINHARES, Maria Yeda & SILVA, Francisco C. Teixeira (1981). *História da Agricultura Brasileira.* Brasiliense Editora, Rio de Janeiro.

LINHARES, Maria Yedda (org) *et alii* (1990). *História Geral do Brasil.* Campus, Editora. 6 Edição, Rio de Janeiro.

MARANHÃO, Ricardo. *O governo JK.* São Paulo:Brasiliense,1981.

MARTINS, José de Souza. *A Militarização da Questão Agrária.* Petrópolis: Vozes,1985.

MELO E SILVA, Alexandra de. *A política externa de JK : Operação Pan-Americana.* Rio de Janeiro: CPDOC,1992.

MYAMOTO, Shiguenoli. 1981. *O pensamento geopolítico Brasileiro (1920-1980)*. Mimeo,USP, São Paulo.

OLIVEIRA, Eliézer R.1976. *As Forças Armadas: política e ideologia no Brasil (1964-1969)*. Vozes, Petrópolis.

______*Militares: Pensamento e Ação Política*. Campinas: Papirus,1987.

PAGE, Joseph. *A Revolução que nunca houve*. Rio de Janeiro: Record, 1972

PATRICK, G. *Fontes de Crescimento na Agricultura Brasileira: o setor de culturas*, in C.R. Contador (org), Tecnologia e desenvolvimento agrícola. Rio de Janeiro, IPEA, 1975.

PEIXOTO, Antonio Carlos. *O Clube Militar e os confrontos no seio das Forças Armadas (1945-1964)* In *Os Partidos Militares no Brasil*. Rouquié, Alain (org) 1980, OLIVEIRA, E.R.& NETO, M.D, Record Editora, Rio de Janeiro.

PEREIRA, Osny D. *A antinomia do acordo militar Brasil-EUA*. Rio de Janeiro, Associação Brasileira de Juristas Democráticos, 15 ab. 1963.

RODRIGUES, José Honório. *Conciliação e reforma no Brasil* .2 Edição .Rio de Janeiro: Nova Fronteira, 1982.

SILVA, Hélio. *Sangue na Areia de Copacabana*. Rio de janeiro: Civilização Brasileira, 1964.

______.1982. *Um tiro no coração*. Civilização Brasileira Editora, Rio de Janeiro.

SKIDMORE, Thomas E. *Brasil: de Getúlio a Castello Branco (1930/1964)*. 4 Edição Rio de Janeiro: Paz e Terra ,1975.

SODRÉ, Nelson Werneck. *Memórias de um Soldado*. Civilização Brasileira Editora, Rio de Janeiro, 1967.

______.1968. *História Militar do Brasil*. Civilização Brasileira, Rio de Janeiro.

______*Formação Histórica do Brasil*.9 Edição. Rio de Janeiro: Civilização Brasileira ,1976

STEPAN, Alfred. *Os Militares na Política*. Rio de Janeiro: Arte Nova,1975

______.1986. *Os militares: da abertura à nova república*. Paz e Terra Editora, Rio de Janeiro.

TOLEDO, Caio Navarro de Toledo. *ISEB-Fábrica de Ideologias*. 2 Edição Campinas:Unicamp,1997

TORRES, Alberto.1933. *A Organização Nacional*. Companhia Editora Nacional, Rio de Janeiro.

TRONCA, Ítalo.1991 . *O Exército e a industrialização entre as armas e Volta Redonda (1930-1942)*. In Fausto, B.(org), HGCB, tomo III, 3 vol. DIFEL, São Paulo.

VELHO, Otávio G (1976). *Capitalismo Autoritário e Campesinato*. Difel Editora, Rio de Janeiro.

VIANNA, Luiz Werneck. *A Revolução Passiva*. Rio de Janeiro: Revan, 1997

VIANA, Oliveira. 1959. *O Ocaso do* Império. José Olympio Editora, 3 Edição, Rio de Janeiro.

______.1974. *Problemas de Organização e Problemas de Direção: o povo e o governo*. Record Editora, 2 edição, Rio de Janeiro.

VINHAS, Moisés. *A Terra, o homem, as reformas*. Rio de Janeiro: Graal,1980

Dissertations
DEBERT, Guita Grin. *A Política do Significado no início dos Anos 60: O Nacionalismo no Instituto Superior de Estudos Brasileiros (ISEB) e na Escola Superior de Guerra(ESG)*.Tese de Doutoramento defendida no IFCH/USP, 1986.

FERRAZ, Francisco César Alves. *A Escola Superior de Guerra e política no Brasil: 1948-1955*. Dissertação de mestrado em História defendida na UNESP, 1994.

ABOUT THE AUTHOR

Graduated in international relations, with a master's degree in sociology and a doctorate in public health, with emphasis on society and the environment. He has experience in defense and security issues and is a professor and researcher (senior) for 15 years, teaching at Brazilian colleges/universities in international relations and political science disciplines, among others. Member of an itinerant chair of transdisciplinarity. He was ad hoc consultant in the area of international cooperation of the Coordination of Improvement of Higher Education Personnel (CAPES), a foundation linked to the Brazilian Ministry of Education (MEC), which works to expand and consolidate *stricto sensu* postgraduate studies (Master's and Ph.D.) in all states of the country. Has articles published in varied Journals. Part-time journalist and founding partner of the Environmental Protection Area Society of Morro do Leme, Rio de Janeiro, Brazil. He is currently a postdoctoral fellow at the Catholic University of Portugal and is a senior researcher at the Center for Philosophical and Humanistic Studies at the University in Braga.